1949

1949

David French

Talonbooks   •   Vancouver   •   1989

Copyright © 1989 David French

published with the assistance of the Canada Council

Talonbooks
201 / 1019 East Cordova Street
Vancouver
British Columbia   V6A 1M8
Canada

Typeset in Baskerville by Pièce de Résistance Ltée; printed and
bound in Canada by Hignell Printed Ltd.

Second Printing: October 1990

Canadian Cataloguing in Publication Data

   French, David, 1939 -
   1949

   A play.
   ISBN 0-88922-266-5

   I. Title.
   PS8561.R44N56 1989   C812'.54   C89-091308-0
   PR9199.3.F74N56 1989

For my son, Gareth

1949 was first produced at the Bluma Appel Theatre, St. Lawrence Centre by the Canadian Stage Company, Toronto, in October 1988 with the following cast:

Jacob Mercer	Michael Hogan
Mary Mercer	Dixie Seatle
Ben Mercer	Darryl Flatman
Billy Mercer	Zachary Bennett
Rachel Mercer	Patricia Hamilton
Wiff Roach	Benedict Campbell
Dot Roach	Brenda Robbins
Jerome McKenzie	Tom Butler
Grace Wilcox	Sherry Bie
Norman Harris	Gordon Jocelyn
Miss Dunn	Shirley Josephs
Doctor Hunter	Neil Vipond
Ned Spencer	Lorne Pardy
April Adams	Lisa Bunting

Directed by Bill Glassco
Set and Costumes by Peter Hartwell
Lighting by Jeffrey Dallas
1949 moved to Manitoba Theatre's Mainstage in November 1988.

"Hurrah for our own native Isle, Newfoundland—
Not a stranger shall hold one inch of her strand:
Her face turns to Britain, her back to the Gulf,
Come near at your peril, Canadian Wolf!"
                        —anti-Confederation song

"Those who wanted confederation may now rejoice and those who opposed it must grin and bear it. But for many there is something that is going out of their hearts, something that will leave a void that will not be easily or quickly filled."
                        —St. John's *Daily News*, April 1, 1949

CHARACTERS

Jacob Mercer
Mary Mercer
Ben Mercer
Billy Mercer
Rachel Mercer
Wiff Roach
Dot Roach
Jerome McKenzie
Grace Wilcox
Norman Harris
Miss Dunn
Doctor Hunter
Ned Spencer
April Adams

SCENE

The dining room, living room, and front porch of the Mercer house in Toronto.

TIME

March 29th, 30th, and 31st, 1949.

Act I

Scene I—late Tuesday afternoon, March 29th, 1949.

Scene II—early that evening.

Act II

Scene I—Wednesday night, March 30th.

Scene II—Thursday night, March 31st.

ACT ONE

Scene I

*The setting is the dining room, living room, and front porch
of a modest but comfortable working-class house in Toronto,
1949. The dining room contains a good oak table and chairs
and a sideboard. On the table at the moment are a bottle of
lemon oil and a rag. In one corner of the room is a small
alcove with a telephone table and telephone. A door leads off
the dining room into the kitchen which is offstage.*

*The living room is furnished with a sturdy chesterfield and
armchair, both with antimacassars. In front of the
chesterfield is a coffee table on which stands a pot of African
violets still in the green paper from the florist shop. Beside the
armchair is a floorlamp with a tasseled shade. An old
wind-up Victrola sits against one wall and beside it a stack
of 78 records. On the mantlepiece rest silver-framed photos of
the family. Next to the fireplace stands a large radio console.
And on the floor is a faded Turkish carpet.*

The hall that leads from the front door to the living room is visible, though not necessarily the front door. Also visible in the hall is a staircase that leads up to the second floor.

A Union Jack hangs from a flagpole on the front porch.

It is about four-thirty on the afternoon of Tuesday, March 29th, 1949.

At rise: RACHEL MERCER, 65, stands beside the coffee table in the living room, peering at a florist's card through a large bone-handled magnifying glass. The fact that she wears her hair pinned back in a bun only emphasizes the no-nonsense air about the woman. On her nose are a pair of wire-rimmed glasses, and on her arm, a black armband.

BEN MERCER, 10, is seated on the top step of the porch, applying shoe polish to a pair of men's black shoes. Beside him is a black brush.

A song plays on the radio.

NED: *off—upstairs*
Mrs. Mercer, where are the aspirins?

RACHEL: *calls upstairs*
They'm in the same place they've been, Ned, since you started boarding here: the medicine chest!

NED: *off*
I can't find them!

RACHEL:
Look again!   *With that she tucks the card into its envelope and sticks it back into the African violets. She crosses into the dining room and replaces the magnifying glass in the sideboard. Then she picks up the lemon oil and rag and begins to polish the oak table. Calls out:*   Did you find them, Ned?

NED: *off*
Not yet!

RACHEL   *to herself*
He couldn't find his nose today if he was Pinnochio.

> *At that moment NORMAN HARRIS, late sixties, enters from the street, carrying a small white enamel pot of chowder. (NOTE: BEN, as do all the people who know NORMAN, raises his voice when talking to the slightly deaf old man.)*

NORMAN:
Hello, Ben.

BEN:
Hi, Mr. Harris.

NORMAN:
How's Billy? Is he okay?

BEN:
Oh, sure.

NORMAN:
That's good . . . Is your grandmother home?

BEN:
She's inside, Mr. Harris. Some flowers just came for Aunt Dot. Granny's probably reading the card.

NORMAN:
Yes, well, I'll just go in.   *He enters the house, calling:*
Rachel, it's me, Norman!

RACHEL: *to herself*
My God, not him again . . . .

NED: *off*
Mrs. Mercer, I found the aspirins!

RACHEL:
Good! Now don't forget to take some!

11

NORMAN:
What's that?　　　*He crosses into the living room.*

RACHEL:　　　*sets down the lemon oil and rag and turns*
　　　off the radio
So what'd you bring us today, Norman? We still haven't
finished those biscuits.

NORMAN:
I was making chowder for supper, I was, and I thought
I'd bring some over for Billy. I know how he likes my
seafood chowder.　　　*Hands her the pot like an offering.*

RACHEL:
That's kind of you, Norman. He can't eat that yet.
Maybe tomorrow.

NORMAN:
I had the scare of my life today, I did. I was down at the
butcher shop and Walt said you'd come in wearing a
black armband. My first thought was Billy.

RACHEL:
Why would you t'ink that?

NORMAN:
Why? Well, he did have his tonsils out two days ago. I
thought something might have happened.

RACHEL:
Not'ing's happened, Norman. He's upstairs reading
comic books . . . I'll just put this is the icebox!　　　*She*
exits into the kitchen.

NORMAN:　　　*calls out*
Even Walt was puzzled, Rachel. He couldn't figure out
why you'd be wearing a mourning band unless someone
passed away. I said, 'Walt, I live next door, and if
anything happened, don't you think I'd know?' He
suggested it was a distant relative, maybe. Or a friend.

RACHEL: *returning*
No one died, Norman. Now I'd like to offer you a cup of tea, but I can't. There's a t'ousand and one t'ings to do before tonight.   *She begins to usher him out.*

NORMAN:
Why? What's happening tonight?

RACHEL:
We'm having company, if you must know. A newspaper in Newfoundland is sending a man here to the house.

NORMAN:
What in the world for?

RACHEL:
They wants to do a piece on a family from back home living in Toronto on the eve of Confederation. Don't ask me why.

NORMAN:
Well, I'll be damned.   *RACHEL ushers him out the front door.*

RACHEL: *appearing on the porch*
That's why I can't sit and chat with you, Norman. Maybe in a day or two.

NORMAN:
How come they chose this family?

RACHEL:
That's a good question, Norman. Maybe because the news reporter was someone we knowed back home. He taught school in those days. Used to go with my daughter-in-law when she was just a girl . . . Now if you'll excuse me, Norman . . .

NORMAN:

Oh, don't mind me. I have to get back anyway. I left the chowder simmering, I did. Well, goodbye, now. Goodbye, Ben. Goodbye, Rachel.   *He grins at RACHEL, then exits down the street.*

Slight Pause.

BEN: *intently brushing a shoe*

Mr. Harris has a crush on you, Granny.

RACHEL:

Don't be foolish. He's just a nosey old goat. And don't be getting shoe polish on your pants, you hear?

BEN:

I won't.

RACHEL:

And mind you don't dirty the laces.

BEN:

I took the laces out.

RACHEL:

Did you, now?

BEN:

I didn't get polish on the soles, either, Granny.

RACHEL:

I never mentioned the soles.

BEN:

You would have.

RACHEL:

Don't be smart . . . And you don't need to wear out the leather. Ned's not going to Buckingham Palace, no odds how he acts.

At that moment DR. HUNTER enters from the street, carrying his black bag. He is in his mid-fifties, dressed in unpressed tweeds, shirt and tie.

DR. HUNTER:
Afternoon, Rachel.

RACHEL:
Afternoon, Doctor. We wasn't expecting you today.

DR. HUNTER:
No, I was in the neighbourhood. Thought I'd drop by and pick up my hat. I left it here the other day . . . So how's your brother, Ben? Is he up and around?

BEN:
He's still in bed, Doctor. Any excuse to get more gingerale.

DR. HUNTER:
Why? Won't he give you any?

BEN:
No, he's stingy.

RACHEL:
Billy keeps marking the bottles. *She and the doctor exchange a smile.* Well, I suppose I'd better fetch your hat.

DR. HUNTER:
No hurry, Rachel. Now that I'm here I may as well look in on young Bill. Has he been eating much?

RACHEL: *letting the doctor precede her into the house*
Doctor, he'd have his tonsils out again, if he could, just to get all that Jell-O and ice cream.

DR. HUNTER: *in the living room*
Something smells good.

RACHEL:
> There's a roast in the oven.

DR. HUNTER:
> The women are in the kitchen, are they?

RACHEL:
> No, Mary had to go out for a spell. She oughtn't to be too long.

DR. HUNTER:
> Dot go with her?

RACHEL:
> Dot? No, I heard her say she might go down to Eaton's. I suppose she'll buy herself a pair of shoes to cheer herself up. She's been having a hard time of it.

DR. HUNTER:
> Yes, I noticed that the other day. She still looked as lovely as ever, though.

> *Just then NED SPENCER rushes down the stairs. He is a young man of twenty-one. At the moment the only clothes he has on are his pants and an undershirt.*

NED:
> Mrs. Mercer, is it okay if I borrow your iron?

RACHEL:
> What? Aren't you dressed yet?

NED:
> I still have to iron me pants and shirt.

RACHEL:
> Well, just don't burn my ironing board. And don't forget to unplug the flatiron.

NED:
> I won't.

DR. HUNTER:
  Big date, Ned?

NED:
  I guess you could say that, Doctor. I'm meeting my girl's
  parents for the first time.

DR. HUNTER:
  That sounds serious.

NED:
  I'd sooner have me foot amputated.   *He exits upstairs.*

DR. HUNTER:
  He doesn't sound too thrilled, does he?

RACHEL:
  Well, you'd never know it, the way he's been carrying
  on. It's a wonder he hasn't shaved off his nose . . . You
  can go up now, Doctor. Billy's in his room.

  > *DR. HUNTER starts for the stairs, carrying his black
  > bag. Suddenly he halts.*

DR. HUNTER:
  By the way, Rachel, I notice you're wearing a black
  armband . . .

RACHEL:
  Save your breath, Doctor. Nobody's died that's close to
  me. The last Mercer to pass away was my husband. I
  buried him in 1937.

DR. HUNTER:
  Then why the . . . ?   *Gestures to indicate the armband.*

RACHEL:
  I'm afraid you'd have to be a Newfoundlander, my son,
  to understand. It's not your fault you was born in
  Canada.

17

DR. HUNTER:
Well, the day after tomorrow, Rachel, we'll all be Canadians. You won't be able to lord it over me then. *He smiles and continues up the stairs.*

RACHEL: *to herself*
Canadian, my foot! *She crosses into the dining room, picks up the bottle of lemon oil and the rag, exiting into the kitchen.*

At that moment DOT ROACH enters from the street, carrying an Eaton's box under one arm and her purse over the other. She is thirty-seven and quite attractive. She wears a hat and coat.

DOT:
Hello, my darling.

BEN:
Hi, Aunt Dot.

DOT:
What? No kiss? *She bends and lets BEN kiss her cheek.* That's better. At your age you don't like to kiss girls, but in a few years you'll appreciate the practice. *She ruffles his hair and enters the house, calling:* Mary! I'm home! *She enters the living room and sets the Eaton's box on the chesterfield. She glances at the African violets as she returns to the hall and hangs up her hat and coat.*

RACHEL enters from the kitchen, carrying a lace tablecloth. She drops it on the dining room table and continues in to the living room.

RACHEL:
Oh, it's you, Dot. I t'ought I heard someone come in . . . I see you've had your hair done.

DOT:
Like it?

RACHEL:
It's lovely, maid.

DOT:
Makes my face look t'inner, don't you t'ink? I bought a
new dress for tonight. Wait till you sees it, Aunt
Rachel.   *She brings the dress from the box and holds it
against her body.*   I've never had a dress this lovely.

RACHEL:
That must've cost you some.

DOT:
What odds? I figured as long as we're getting our picture
in the paper, I might as well look my best. One day I'll
point to that picture: 'That appeared in the paper back
home the day Newfoundland became the tenth province
of Canada.'

RACHEL:
Yes, All Fools' Day.

DOT: *folding the dress back into the box*
Well, not everyone feels that way, Aunt Rachel. Some of
us t'inks it's a good idea.

RACHEL: *testily*
Then why did half of Newfoundland vote against it?

DOT:
Half of it didn't.

RACHEL:
Almost half. It was only a few t'ousand votes that made
the difference.

DOT: *steps back and appraises her*
You know what suddenly puzzles me, Aunt Rachel? Now
that I t'inks of it?

RACHEL:
  What?

DOT:
  Why did you agree to let Mr. McKenzie come to the
  house to write a piece on Confederation? That seems odd,
  considering how you feels.

RACHEL:
  I couldn't stop him, could I? It's not *my* house.

DOT:
  No, but it was you he spoke to the other day on the
  phone. You could've refused him and nobody here
  would've been the wiser. Why didn't you?

RACHEL:
  I'm not myself on the phone. In person I might have.
  Besides, didn't I put this armband on today to let him
  know which side I'm on?

DOT:
  Maybe. I still t'inks you're up to somet'ing, Aunt
  Rachel. I can feel it in my bones.   *By now BEN has
  finished with the shoes. He takes the brush, the tin of polish, and
  the shoes and starts inside the house, slamming the front door.*

RACHEL:
  I wish he wouldn't slam that door.   *As BEN runs up
  the stairs, DOT takes the card from the African violets.*
  Don't run up the stairs, Ben, you'll trip and hurt yourself!

BEN: *off*
  No, I won't!

RACHEL:
  If I says white, he says black. One of these days he'll fall
  and bite his tongue in half . . .   *She turns to find DOT
  reading the card.*   Oh, yes, I forgot. Those came not
  ten minutes ago.

DOT:
Did you read the card?

RACHEL: *insulted*
Indeed I didn't. Wiff writes with such a tiny scrawl,
you'd need a magnifying glass. *She straightens the
antimacassars on the armchair.* Whatever it says, he
must be some lonesome. Last week he sent roses, today
it's African violets.

DOT:
Lonesome or not, I'm not going back to him till he shapes
up. I told him that and I means it. *She gathers up the
Eaton's box.* He could buy me all the diamonds in
Africa, it won't change my mind one bit. *She exits
upstairs.*

RACHEL: *to herself*
Poor old Wiff. He's no match for that one.

Just then BEN comes tearing down the stairs.

RACHEL:
Didn't I just tell you not to run down those stairs?

BEN:
No. You said not to run *up* them.

RACHEL:
Don't be smart . . . *As BEN edges towards the front
door.* Where you off to?

BEN:
Ned gave me a dime. I'm going down to Robertson's for
a rootbeer milkshake.

RACHEL:
You'll spoil your supper.

BEN:
No, I won't. *Starts to exit.*

RACHEL:

Stop contradicting me! And don't slam that door!
It slams behind him.   Might as well plead with a rock
rolling down a hill.   *She enters the dining room and
straightens the tablecloth.*

    *DR. HUNTER returns down the stairs, carrying his black
bag.*

DR. HUNTER:

I think Ned is definitely the artistic type. I just had to
show him how to iron his pants.

RACHEL:

He's not having much luck, though, with his stories.
Another came back in the mail today.

DR. HUNTER:

A good thing he works at the Post Office. At least he can
save on stamps.

RACHEL:

How's Billy?

DR. HUNTER:

Oh, he's fine, Rachel. I told him he could go back to
school tomorrow. He wanted to know why Rickie Doyle
was off a whole week when Dr. Nutt took *his* tonsils out.

RACHEL:

Yes, well, Rickie had his out in the hospital, not on the
kitchen table.

DR. HUNTER:

I told him that. I said, 'Rickie was a sick boy, Bill. Rickie
didn't come out of the ether and ask to have his tonsils in
a Mason jar, now did he?'

    *NED comes down the stairs, distraught. He is wearing a
white silk shirt, unbottoned.*

NED:

This was bound to happen today, Mrs. Mercer! First, I have the best story I've ever written rejected by *The Atlantic Monthly*; then that bulldog ripped a hole in me mailbag! And now this!

RACHEL:

Why? What is it now?

NED:

This shirt was a birthday present from April! It's pure silk! I've only worn it once! And you know what kind of an idiot I am, Mrs. Mercer?

RACHEL:

Slow to get to the p'int.

NED:

I burnt it! *He whips off the shirt and holds it up, revealing a hole in the back of the shirt the size and shape of the iron. He plunges his arm through it.* I can't go now! April wants to show it to her folks! If I show up without it, she'll think I don't like her present!

RACHEL:

Well, if you don't show up at all, she'll t'ink you don't like her parents. Make up your mind.

NED:

I already have. I'll call and say I'm going for a tetanus shot. I'll say that bulldog bit me.

DR. HUNTER:

Ned, they'll be insulted if you don't show up. They probably just want to look you over.

NED:

Tough! I'm not going to sit there and let them cross-examine me for two hours! I'm not a criminal!
He storms into the dining room.

RACHEL:
No one said you was.

NED: *picks up the phone, listens, then slams down the receiver*
That bloody woman is always on the line! Always
babbling on how cute the iceman is in his rubber apron!
*He sits at the dining room table and puts his head in his
hands.* You know how much I make at the Post
Office, Doctor? Eighteen hundred dollars a year. You
think that's going to impress her father? . . .

DR. HUNTER:
Look, would you mind leaving us, Rachel? I'd like a few
words alone with Ned.

RACHEL: *starts for the kitchen*
I suppose I could check the roast. Mary'd have a fit if I
burnt it. *She exits.*

DR. HUNTER: *crosses to the archway*
So, Ned, what does this girl do. Does she work for a
living?

NED:
She's a dance instructor at Arthur Murray's.

DR. HUNTER:
Is that how you met her? You signed up for classes?

NED: *rises*
No, I deliver the mail there. Two months ago I had a
registered letter, which April signed for. That's when I
first saw her. The same day I went back and signed up for
five thousand dollars worth of classes.

DR. HUNTER:
Five thousand dollars!

NED:
Well, for that I get a thousand hour course, plus two free
hours of instruction each month for the rest of me life.

DR. HUNTER:
What are you, Ned, a slow learner?

NED: *crosses into the living room, frantic and desperate*
The trouble is there's this other instructor, this Fred
Noseworthy, who's always sniffing around her. Still,
she'd be better off with someone like Fred, even if he does
fancy himself. At least he can waltz without counting! . . .

   Slight Pause.

DR. HUNTER:
All right, Ned. Now this has nothing to do with a silk
shirt, and we both know it.

NED:
Why do you say that?

DR. HUNTER:
Why? Because you were so taken with this girl you were
willing to mortage your life just to be around her. That
sort of man doesn't throw in the towel over a hole in a
shirt.

NED:
I guess not.

DR. HUNTER:
So what is it then?

NED:
I've lied to her, Doctor.

DR. HUNTER:
We all lie on occasion, Ned.

NED:
I've been lying to her all along. I'm a fraud.

DR. HUNTER:
Why? What have you done?

NED:

    I told her I was Irish!

DR. HUNTER: *amused*

    You probably do have some Irish blood. Didn't a lot of
the Irish settle in Newfoundland?

NED:

    This is different. It all started that first class I took. When
I went in, she was sitting on the floor engrossed in this
book, *Drums Under The Windows*, by Sean O'Casey.
    With an Irish accent.   'Hey,' I said, 'did you read
O'Casey's other book, *Pictures In The Hallway*? It made
me homesick for Dublin.'

DR. HUNTER:

    Why the hell did you do that, Ned? Why?

NED:

    I don't know! Maybe I figured she was Irish herself! Or
that Ireland held a special place in her imagination! It
doesn't matter now!   *He sits, looking like a cornered
animal.*

DR. HUNTER:

    All right, Ned, I'll tell you what you're going to do. You
listening?

NED:

    What?

DR. HUNTER:

    First, you go upstairs and put on another shirt, and when
she asks tonight why you're not wearing the silk shirt she
gave you, you simply tell her the truth.

NED:

    What? That I'm too stupid to iron a shirt?

DR. HUNTER:
That'll do for starters. Then later on, Ned, you take her
aside and tell her the rest.

NED:
She'll never trust me again.

DR. HUNTER:
That's the chance you have to take. Of course if you're
not serious about this girl . . .

NED:
I am, Doctor. I want to marry her.

DR. HUNTER:
In that case you have to meet her parents. Now go on
before she calls up and wants to know where you are.

NED: *crossing to the stairs*
There's no way she'll call here, Doctor. I told her we
don't have a phone . . . Anyway, thanks. I just hope for
my sake you're right.   *He exits upstairs.*

DR. HUNTER: *to himself*
So do I, Ned. So do I . . .   *Suddenly he fixes on the pot
of African violets as though he's just noticed it for the first time.
With a furtive look around, he crosses quickly to the coffee table and
removes the card from its envelope. Just as he is reading the card,
RACHEL enters from the kitchen, carrying a stack of dinner plates
which she sets down on the table. Quickly, the doctor replaces the
card in the envelope and tucks it back inside the African violets.
Then he retrieves his black bag and crosses to the archway.*
I'm leaving now, Rachel. I'll see myself out.

RACHEL:
Let me get my purse, Doctor.

DR. HUNTER:
That's okay. Maybe next time you can spare a bottle of
that wine Jacob made. I'm all out.

RACHEL:
I t'ought you said that parsnip wine almost blinded you?

DR. HUNTER:
It did. I'm using it now to sterilize my instruments . . .
Well, tell Mary I'm sorry I missed her. Oh, yes, and tell
Dot I hope she's feeling better.

RACHEL:
I'm surprised, Doctor, you didn't bump into her. She
came in when you was upstairs with Billy.

DR. HUNTER:
Did she? I didn't hear her.

RACHEL:
Oh, and don't forget your hat, it's in the hall. I don't
want to be chasing you down the street. Goodbye, now.
I'd best set the table before the stampede begins . . .
     DR. HUNTER crosses into the hall and gets his hat.
Oh, by the way, Doctor, how'd it go with Ned?

DR. HUNTER:
I can't be sure, Rachel. Advice is no more an exact
science than medicine.   *He glances up the stairs, then
sets his fedora on the top of the gramophone. He then walks out onto
the porch and down the steps, stopping to breathe in the day.*

     At that moment DOT comes hurrying down the stairs.

DOT:
Aunt Rachel, Ned said the doctor was here. He hasn't
left, has he?

RACHEL: *crosses to the archway*
Just a second ago, maid.   *Notices the fedora on the
gramophone.*   Don't tell me he forgot that hat!

     *DOT snatches the fedora and rushes out to the porch, just as
the doctor is walking away.*

DOT:

> Dr. Hunter, your hat!

> *The doctor returns to the steps. He fixes on DOT, then
> smiles. Reaches up for the hat.*

DR. HUNTER:

> Thanks, Dot. I don't know what's wrong with me lately.
> I'm getting more and more forgetful.   *He slaps the
> fedora on the back of his head. RACHEL exits into the kitchen.*
> Dot, I wish I had a camera. You'd make a lovely
> picture in that light.

DOT:

> I wish I felt lovely, Doctor.

DR. HUNTER:

> I suppose you miss your own home. It's hard living under
> someone else's roof, even a sister's.

DOT:

> That's what I wanted to talk to you about, Doctor. Do
> you have a minute?

DR. HUNTER:

> Oh, I'm in no big rush. I was just going home to make
> supper and listen to *Fibber McGee and Molly.*   *He sets
> down his black bag and removes his fedora.*   What can I
> do for you?

DOT:

> It's about Wiff . . .

DR. HUNTER:

> What about him?

DOT:

> I just wondered . . . Well, I wondered if he'd been to see
> you again. He said he intended to . . .

DR. HUNTER:
    No, I haven't seen Wiff for at least a month. That was
    before you moved out. He wanted to know about the
    sperm test, so I explained it.

DOT:
    Why won't he do it, Doctor? Why? I won't go back till he
    does. I've told him that.

DR. HUNTER:
    Maybe he's just embarrassed, Dot. Or maybe he's afraid
    of what he'll find out.

DOT:
    He kicked up such a fuss when I first suggested the test.
    But I always expected he'd come around in the end.

DR. HUNTER:
    Maybe he needs time, Dot.

DOT:
    Doctor, I'm t'irty-seven years old, I don't have time. I
    waited six years for Wiff to come home from the War so's
    we could start a family. He's been back four years now,
    Doctor. Four years.

DR. HUNTER:
    I understand.

DOT:
    He calls, he sends flowers; he even sent me a telegram.
    All he has to do to get me back is go to the Clinic. It's a lot
    easier for the man to be tested first.

DR. HUNTER:
    I explained all that.

DOT:
    Sometimes I wonders if he even wants children. Maybe
    the War changed him, Doctor. In some ways he's never
    been the same.

DR. HUNTER:
> There are men, of course, who've come back from the
> War unable to have children. Men who were never
> wounded. Men who were perfectly healthy before that.
> We think it might have something to do with the
> psychological effects of combat . . . Look, maybe what
> the two of you need to do is talk it out. A lot of problems
> get solved that way, simply by . . .

DOT: *cutting in*
> No, Doctor, we've talked enough. I just t'ought if you
> saw him again you could make him understand how I
> feels. I don't seem to be able to . . .   *The doctor says*
> *nothing.*   Well, t'anks for listening. I won't keep you
> any longer . . .   *She starts for the door, then turns.*
>   I don't t'ink he understands how much I wants a child.
> You're a man, Doctor. Would you behave that way?
> *The doctor says nothing. DOT nods and starts into the house.*

DR. HUNTER: *to himself*
> No, Dot. No, I wouldn't.   *Angrily, he slaps his fedora*
> *on his head, snatches up his black bag, and exits down the street.*

> *BILLY MERCER, aged 9, comes down the stairs in his*
> *pajamas, passing DOT as she goes upstairs. He enters the*
> *dining room just as RACHEL comes out of the kitchen with*
> *the cutlery.*

RACHEL:
> Get back in bed.

BILLY:
> The doctor says I can get up. He says if I stay in bed, I'll
> miss school on Thursday.

RACHEL:
> Is that when your school sings 'Ode to Newfoundland'?

BILLY:
> Yeah.

RACHEL:
Do you know what that song is, Billy?

BILLY:
No . . .

RACHEL:
It's the national anthem of the country you was born in.
Do you know the words?   *BILLY shakes his head.*
No, I didn't t'ink so. Go on, now. Go get dressed.
We'm having company after supper.

BILLY:
I want to see my tonsils.

RACHEL:
All right, but leave them in the icebox. And if you wants
more Jell-O, eat it in the kitchen. I'm setting the table.
     She begins to set out the cutlery.   Now scat.

*BILLY exits into the kitchen just as MARY MERCER
enters from the street, her purse over her shoulder. MARY is
forty-one, slender and very attractive. Her shoulder-length
black hair is permed and she wears no make-up. She enters
the house and crosses into the living room, sitting on the arm
of the armchair as though catching her breath, her purse
clutched to her breast.*

*From the dining room RACHEL has seen MARY enter.
She sets down the last of the cutlery and enters the living
room. For a moment RACHEL watches MARY, almost
afraid to intrude.*

RACHEL: *finally*
You just missed the doctor, Mary. He dropped in to pick
up his hat.

MARY:
Sorry, Aunt Rachel. I never expected to be this long. Did
you peel the potatoes?

RACHEL:

 Yes, and the roast is on. Jacob's not home yet. Oh, and
 Jerome called. He's staying at the Royal York Hotel.
 They arrived last night. Took them fourteen hours to fly
 here.

MARY:

 They? Who's they?

RACHEL:

 He never said. Just that they'd be over at eight and not to
 go to any fuss on their account. I said we wouldn't, then
 dusted the house from top to bottom.

MARY:

 I'm not so sure this is a good idea, Aunt Rachel. I'm not
 in much of a mood to have my picture taken. Damn that
 woman! I had to walk around the block to cool off.
 She rises and paces.

DOT: *coming down the stairs*
 What's wrong, Mary? What is it?

MARY

 Didn't Aunt Rachel tell you?

RACHEL:

 No, I figured Dot had enough on her mind. She'd just get
 more upset.   *Sits in the armchair.*

DOT:

 Upset about what? What's happened?

MARY:

 Ben got the strap today.

DOT:

 The strap?

MARY:
>That's where I've been, down to the school. His teacher gave him seven whacks on each hand with that big leather strap. I saw it hanging on a hook just inside her door.

DOT:
>I was right about her, wasn't I? I said she had nasty eyes. Even her mouth looks like a wound. Jesus, I'd like to run down there and rip that orange wig off her head! Remember how she was tugging on it the night we went to the Home and School meeting?

RACHEL:
>She wears a wig?

MARY:
>I said, 'Miss Dunn, what could a ten-year-old possibly do to deserve that kind of punishment?' 'I have to make an example of trouble-makers,' she said, 'or I'd never be able to teach.'

DOT:
>What did you say?

MARY:
>I said, 'That wouldn't be much of a loss, Miss Dunn.'

DOT:
>You didn't!

MARY:
>'That's easy for you to say, Mrs. Mercer. You don't have to face t'irty children five days a week.' 'No,' I said, 'I don't. But I have two of my own seven days a week, and I've never laid a hand on either one. And if you ever touches my son again,' I said, 'I'll march down here, take that grey strap off the wall, and smack you across the face with it.'

DOT:
>You didn't!

MARY:
    I did.

RACHEL:
    What was it he got the strap for? Was he talking back?

MARY:
    No, he was fighting.

DOT:
    Fighting?

RACHEL:
    What? In class?

MARY:
    Him and that Italian boy, Albert Sanilosi. The one they
    calls Junior . . . Miss Dunn had hung a map of
    Newfoundland over the blackboard. She asked Ben to go
    up and p'int out where he was born; he couldn't.

DOT:
    No wonder. He was only six when he left.

MARY:
    Junior said somet'ing to Ben under his breath, and Ben
    hit him. I guess Junior fell against Miss Dunn and
    knocked her flat on her backside.

DOT:
    I'd like to have seen that.

RACHEL:
    What was it Junior whispered?

MARY:
    She didn't know. And neither boy would tell. So she gave
    them both the strap . . .

RACHEL: *rises*

Oh, well, no odds. I don't suppose much harm's been done. The strap may have stung his hands, Mary, but it didn't damage his tongue. Ten times today I've wanted to whack him myself. *She exits into the kitchen.*

MARY and DOT exchange a look, then break into giggles. DOT crosses and embraces MARY.

DOT:

The way she talks, you'd never know he was her favorite.

MARY:

Don't let Billy hear you say that.

DOT:

She's right, though, not to make too much of it. Ben's probably forgotten it already.

MARY:

It's hard to know with Ben. He's like his father, he keeps a lot inside.

DOT:

Jacob? What does Jacob ever keep to himself? He's the first to let you know exactly how he feels.

MARY:

Not always. I don't t'ink he wants Jerome here tonight, but he'd never admit it.

DOT:

Why? Has he said anyt'ing?

MARY:

No, not a word. Not even to Aunt Rachel, and she's the one who invited him here. He wouldn't want to let on he was jealous.

DOT:

What? After all these years?

36

MARY:

Strange as it seems.

DOT:

Well, I've never been with another man to upset Wiff. Wiff was my first.

MARY:

Go on with you. I've never been with Jerome, either, in the sense you means it.

DOT:

You and Jerome didn't . . . ?

MARY:

Indeed we didn't.

DOT:

But you was engaged to him.

MARY:

Only that summer I was seventeen. And he never laid a hand on me. Not that he didn't try. No, Jacob's the only man I've ever slept with.

BILLY enters from the kitchen and crosses into the living room.

BILLY:

Mom, Dr. Hunter said I can go back to school tomorrow.

MARY:

Did he, now?

BILLY:

Can I take my tonsils with me, Mom? Can I?

MARY:

We'll see.

BILLY:
> Oh, boy! Wait'll the kids see those!   *He exits upstairs.*

> *At that moment JACOB MERCER enters from the street,
> carrying his black lunchpail in one hand and a rolled-up
> newspaper in the other. JACOB is forty-one, a solidly built
> man of enormous vitality. He wears a cap, slacks, and a
> windbreaker.*

NORMAN: *off*
> Hello, Jacob!

JACOB:
> Oh, hello, Norman! A grand day!

NORMAN: *off*
> What's that?

JACOB:
> I SAID IT'S A GRAND DAY!

DOT:
> Jacob's home.

MARY:
> Don't let on to Jacob that Ben got the strap. I'll tell him
> myself later.

> *JACOB enters the house, removing his cap and windbreaker.
> He hangs them on the hatrack and enters the living room.*

JACOB:
> Norman needs a hearing-horn the size of that Victrola the
> dog sits in front of on RCA Victor records. Hello, Dot.
> *Tosses the newspaper into the armchair.*   Hello,
> Mary.

MARY:
> You're late.

JACOB:

I was t'irsty. I dropped into the Oakwood for a quick one.

DOT:

Was Wiff there?

JACOB:

No, but I met this other fellow. He said, 'Where you from?' I said, 'Newfoundland.' He said, 'I met a Newfoundlander once. Fellow name of O'Leary from Red Rocks. Don't suppose you knows him?' 'No,' I said, 'I never met him. For one t'ing,' I said, 'Red Rocks is on the west coast about five hundred miles from where I lived. For Christ's sake, man,' I said, Newfoundland is the sixteenth largest island in the world with a coastline of six t'ousand miles. You might as well ask me if I knows Norma Sludge from Dildo.' The damn fool!

DOT: *meaning his lunchpail*
Here, I'll take that, Jacob.   *To MARY.*   I'll give Aunt Rachel a hand. And I might as well water these, I suppose.   *She takes the pot of African violets and starts for the kitchen.*

JACOB: *to DOT*
Tell Mother Norman's out on his porch just waiting to pounce on her!

RACHEL: *off*
I heard that!

        DOT exits.

JACOB:

By God, here's someone *I*'d like to pounce on.

MARY:

Go on with you.   *He tries to embrace her.*   Stop it, now. What if someone walks in?

39

JACOB:

What odds? Can't a man kiss his wife?   *He continues to get amorous.*

MARY: *mildly rebuking him*
Stop it, I said. My God.

JACOB:

What's wrong?

MARY:

There's not'ing wrong. What's got into you?

JACOB:

I could ask you the same question. You haven't been the same since you had your hair done.

MARY:

That's not true.

JACOB:

Isn't it?

MARY:

No.

JACOB:

Then what was that all about last night? I suppose I imagined it?

MARY:

I was tired.

JACOB:

Not too tired to rush off to the Beauty Parlour yesterday.

MARY:

Look, why don't you just sit down and read your paper? You won't be so cranky once you've eaten.

JACOB:
>I'm not cranky, damnit. Mother gets cranky, I gets cross.
>There's a difference.   *He sits in the armchair and opens*
>*his newspaper.*

>>*NED comes down the stairs. He is wearing a suit and tie,*
>>*his hair slicked down.*

NED: *to MARY*
>How do I look, Mrs. Mercer?

JACOB: *glances up*
>Like you owned your own Funeral Parlour. What's that,
>Ned, a new suit?

NED: *testily*
>No, and the shoes aren't new, either.

MARY:
>You looks smart, Ned.

JACOB:
>I see you got your hair cut, too. All dolled up to get your
>picture in the *Evening Telegram*, is that it? If I was you, I
>wouldn't sit down to supper, you'll crease your pants.

NED:
>Who said I was getting my picture taken? Did I say that?

MARY:
>Pay him no heed, Ned.

NED:
>Well, Jesus!

MARY: *to JACOB*
>He won't be here for supper. April invited him over to
>meet her parents.

JACOB:

April? I notice we never get to meet her, never mind her parents. Why is that, Ned? You ashamed of her or ashamed of us?

NED: *ignoring JACOB—To MARY.*

I don't know how late I'll be, Mrs. Mercer. I took my key, just in case. *RACHEL enters from the kitchen with cloth napkins which she begins to fold and set on the dining room table.*

MARY:

Yes, go on, Ned. This has not'ing to do with you. Have a good time. *NED exits. MARY studies JACOB a moment.* Maybe we never should've invited him, Jacob. Jerome, that is. I wish your mother had never agreed to it. *RACHEL stops and listens.*

JACOB:

Why do you say that? Don't tell me you'm not curious to see how he looks after all these years? I'm sure he's curious about you.

MARY:

I just meant…

JACOB:

What?

MARY:

Forget it. Read your paper. *She enters the dining room to find RACHEL busy with the napkins. She starts for the kitchen, then stops.* Oh, by the way, Aunt Rachel, remember that Gerald Babcock who teaches at Ben's school? The one who coaches the baseball team?

RACHEL:

Poor Gerald. Back home we all t'ought he was simple-minded.

MARY:

You wouldn't say that now. I saw him in the hall today. He had the Newfoundland flag over his door, and he had on a black armband just like yours. *JACOB reacts.*

RACHEL:

Did he, now? Well, I'll have to write his mother and tell her what a loyal Newfoundlander he turned out to be. Not like some I could name. *This towards JACOB.*

MARY grins and shakes her head, exiting into the kitchen. JACOB slaps down his newspaper, rises, and crosses to the archway.

JACOB:

Take that off your arm.

RACHEL:

That I won't.

JACOB:

You'll look some foolish having your picture taken with that on.

RACHEL:

I'll wear what I wants. I might even put on a sour face. And if you was more like Gerald Babcock, you'd do the same.

JACOB:

Gerald Babcock hasn't the brains of a baseball bat. If he was back home, he'd be raising a black flag like those other damn fools, and marching in that mock funeral tomorrow in St. John's.

RACHEL:

Yes, and if your father was alive, he'd be marching along with him. No mistake.

JACOB:

Like hell he would.

RACHEL:

Then you didn't know your father, my son.
Indicates the armband. This is for him as much as for myself.

JACOB:

Go on. Father never had two cents to rub together. He was like the other poor people: no better than a slave to the Water Street merchants. And now his wife's taking sides with the very ones who milked us dry for hundreds of years.

RACHEL:

Well, let me tell you about your own father, Jacob. First and foremost he was a Newfoundlander, and a proud one. His family had lived on the bare rock of Conception Bay for hundreds of years—since before George I of England. Your father built that house you and your own kids was born in—built it with his own two hands from lumber he cut in the woods—built it on the very spot his grandfather's house once stood. Oh, your father may not have had two cents to call his own, but by God, he knowed who he was. He'd never have put his mark on a ballot that gave away his birthright. The way some did last summer, just to get the baby bonuses and old age pensions.

JACOB:

For Christ's sake, maybe they wanted to save enough for a decent funeral. A lot of those people have never seen real money.

RACHEL:

Then a case could be made for Judas Iscariot, couldn't it? Perhaps Judas never saw silver before.

JACOB:

There's no use talking to you, is there? *He starts to turn away.*

44

RACHEL:

Look at your two sons, Jacob. Billy'd be happy to j'in
Canada just to get the medallion the school's handing out
on T'ursday. He don't even know the words to his own
national anthem.

JACOB:

He's nine years old, Mother. How many Canadian kids
his age could tell you the words to 'O Canada'?

RACHEL:

Well, Ben's a year older. At least he ought to be able to
tell on a map where he comes from.

JACOB:

What's you talking about?

RACHEL:

Today his teacher asked him to show the class where
Coley's P'int was to. He had no more idea than poor
Norman next door.

JACOB:

Who told you that?

RACHEL:

Mary did.

JACOB:

I heard her say she was down to the school. What was she
doing there?

RACHEL:

That's not the p'int. The p'int is he should know about
those t'ings. He should know where he comes from and
be proud of it. The way his grandfather was. And he
ought to be taught that a black wreath on a door is not
only for someone who's died. He's old enough to know
there's more than one kind of grief in the heart!
And with that she exits into the kitchen.

JACOB stands for a moment looking after her. Then he sits down in the armchair, a little subdued, and begins to read his newspaper. At the same time BEN runs on from the street. He enters the house, this time not slamming the door. He tiptoes down the hall and starts up the stairs.

JACOB: *without glancing around*
    Come here a moment, Ben.   *Puts down his paper.*

BEN:
    Oh, hi, Dad . . .   *He edges into the room.*

JACOB:
    Tell me: what was your mother doing down at your school today?

BEN:
    Didn't she tell you?

JACOB:
    No, she didn't.

BEN:
    So what you want to know is what Mom was doing down at my school?

JACOB:
    Yes.

BEN:
    I guess she wanted to talk to my teacher, Miss Dunn.

JACOB:
    What about?

BEN:
    What about?

JACOB:
    Yes.

BEN: *beat*
   I can't tell you.

JACOB:
   Why not?

BEN:
   It's a secret, Dad.

JACOB:
   You can tell me.

BEN:
   Then it won't be a secret.

JACOB:
   Don't you like to tell secrets, Ben? I always did.

BEN:
   I don't.

JACOB: *studies him*
   All right, my son, I won't ask you again. Go on, now. Go
   get cleaned up for supper . . .   *As BEN heads for the*
   stairs.   Oh, there is one other t'ing you can do for
   me, Ben.

BEN:
   What?

JACOB:
   You knows that Atlas we bought you for Christmas?
   Bring it down when you comes. There's a certain place
   on the map I'd like to p'int out.

   Blackout.

Scene II

It is early the same evening, about seven-thirty. The porch light is on, and the African violets are back on the coffee table, minus the green wrapping.

DOT is alone on stage, dancing to a tango record that plays on the gramophone. She looks stunning in her new dress, and she knows it. And this confidence shows in the strong energy of her movement . . . .

MARY comes down the stairs in an equally lovely dress, as nervous as a girl at her first prom. DOT stops dancing and studies her.

MARY: *finally*
    Why? Don't I look all right?

DOT:
Maid, I've seen snaps of Mother at your age—you could
be sisters. And you knows how beautiful she was.

MARY:
You'd say that, Dot, if my slip was showing. Button me
up.

DOT: *as she buttons the back of MARY's dress,*
MARY pats her hair
Stop fidgeting. You're worse than the kids.

MARY:
I can't help it . . . What time is it?

DOT:
Around seven-t'irty . . . There. Now sit down and don't
say a word. *She pushes MARY down on the arm of the*
armchair and takes her lipstick and compact from her purse.

MARY:
No. No lipstick.

DOT:
You've never worn it. It'll give some colour to your face
and spice to your life. *She runs the lipstick over*
MARY's lips. There. That's better. *She hands*
MARY a tissue which MARY presses to her mouth.
Maid, you looks like a bonafide movie star. *Hands*
MARY the compact mirror. See for yourself.

MARY: *examining herself*
Just so long as I don't look foolish. Oh, Dot, I don't want
to disapp'int him somehow. Is that vain of me? *She*
returns the mirror.

DOT:
No. He hasn't seen you in twenty-t'ree years. You don't
want him to say to himself, My God, I'm some glad
Jacob Mercer stole *her* away. *She crosses and shuts off*
the gramophone.

MARY:

I was just a girl when he saw me last. Now I'm forty-one years old. The mother of two children.

DOT:

And more lovely than you was then.

MARY:

Remember that time we caught a glimpse of him? The day I went with you to St. John's to see Wiff off to War?

DOT:

Yes, April of 1940.

MARY:

I can still see the Newfoundland Regiment march out of the C.L.B. Armoury at nine that Sunday morning, heading down to the train station near the harbour. That was some sight.

DOT:

The parade was led by the brass band from the Mount Cashel Boys' Orphanage. Remember?

MARY:

Yes, you had Ben in your arms, and we ran alongside, waving.

DOT:

There wasn't too many in church that morning.

MARY:

The crowds lined the way and cheered. Remember that?

DOT:

I remembers Wiff tripping over the heels of the man ahead. Too busy looking for me, the slouch.

MARY:

That's when I spied Jerome. At that time I hadn't seen him in fourteen years. Not since that August night in 1926 . . .

DOT:

'There's Jerome McKenzie,' you said. 'The man I almost married.'

MARY:

I noticed he had a small moustache. There was somet'ing else that was different about him, too, and then I realized what it was.

DOT:

What?

MARY:

A kind of pride. It showed in the way he marched, his chin stuck out, his eyes ahead, more like an officer than a rich man's son. Until that moment I'd always remembered him at twenty years of age, and the look on his face the night I gave him back his ring . . .

BEN bursts in from the kitchen, followed by BILLY. Both kids are dressed up. BEN clutches a Mason jar containing BILLY's tonsils, and BILLY has a Classics Illustrated comic book in his hand.

MARY: *to DOT*
What now?

BEN: *dashing around the dining room table*
I'll give you back your tonsils if you give me *Hiawatha*.

BILLY:

No.

BEN:

Tough. Then you're not getting them.   *He runs into the living room with BILLY chasing him.*

BILLY:
Mom, tell Ben to give me back my tonsils.

BEN:
He won't give me the Classic comic book, Mom.

BILLY: *to MARY*
I haven't finished it yet.

MARY:
If you two don't stop, I'll send you straight to bed. Ben, give your brother back his tonsils. Billy, give Ben the comic book.

BILLY:
But, Mom . . .

MARY:
No buts. Just do as I says.   *They exchange the comic book and Mason jar, reluctantly.*

BILLY: *to BEN*
Stupid!

BEN:
Idiot!

> *BILLY returns to the kitchen. BEN takes his jacket from the hall closet and exits onto the porch. He slips on the jacket, sits on the top step, and begins to read* The Song of Hiawatha.

MARY:
Kids. My God.

DOT:
I'd be only too happy to take them off your hands. Anytime you're fed up, just let me know.

MARY:
> You'll have a child of your own one of these days. You'll
> see. You just have to get Wiff to the Clinic.

DOT:
> Sometimes I wonders . . . I had another one of those
> dreams the other night, Mary.

MARY:
> Oh?

DOT:
> This time I was running down the aisle of a large church,
> and on the altar was a big glass jar with a baby inside
> floating in water.

MARY:
> A baby?

DOT:
> It was looking at me, and its eyes shone like emeralds . . .
> Just then the jar tips and begins to tumble towards the
> floor, all in slow motion.

MARY:
> And all this time you're running towards it?

DOT:
> Yes. Only now I run faster and faster, reaching out my
> arms, straining to catch the jar as it spins and tumbles
> towards the floor . . .

MARY:
> And?

DOT:
> That's all I remembers. I woke up in a sweat . . . All day
> long, maid, I kept seeing that jar on the altar, and the
> eyes of that child like bits of green fire . . .

At that moment WIFF ROACH appears on the street. He is in his early forties. He wears a fedora and a suit with a black mourning tie.

NORMAN: *off*
Hello there, Wiff! They're all home tonight except Ned!

DOT: *to MARY*
What's Wiff doing here?

WIFF:
Norman, my son, if you'd been there the day Our Saviour stepped up to deliver the Sermon on the Mount, there'd be no Christianity! 'HERE COMES JESUS THE MESSIAH!' The poor man would have turned crimson and slunk back into the bullrushes!

DOT: *to MARY*
Listen to that. I suppose he's had a whiskey to summon up his courage.

WIFF:
Hello, Ben. Captain McKenzie arrive yet?

BEN:
He's supposed to be here at eight, Uncle Wiff.

WIFF:
How about your Aunt Dot? Is she home?

BEN:
She's inside with Mom. You want me to tell her you're here?

WIFF:
Would you, my son?

BEN:
Sure.   *Yells.*   AUNT DOT, UNCLE WIFF'S HERE!

MARY: *to DOT*
He's learning that from Norman.

WIFF:
No odds, my precious, I'll just announce myself.
Starts for the front door.

MARY:
Dot, you can't just turn him away, he's your husband.

DOT:
Leave me alone with him, Mary. I'll deal with Wiff in my
own way.

> *MARY nods and exits upstairs. DOT crosses to the
> gramophone, winds it, then puts the arm back on the tango
> record. The music begins, and DOT dances to it.*

> *Hat in hand, WIFF enters the house. He walks into the
> living room and watches DOT as she dances with her back to
> him.*

WIFF: *finally*
Hello, Dot!

DOT: *stops dancing and turns, feigning surprise*
Oh, it's you, Wiff.

WIFF:
Why? Who was you expecting? Fred Astaire or
Valentino?

DOT: *angrily*
All right, I tried to be civil to you, in spite of the fact I told
you not to come here! What is it you wants?

WIFF:
Let me catch my breath, duckie. I'm no sooner in the
door than you spits at me like a cat.

DOT: *resumes dancing*
Then don't make fun of me. It's hard to dance the tango
by yourself, you needs a man to lead.

WIFF:
I never meant to make fun, Dot, I swear. In fact, you
looks lovelier than you have in years. That's a new dress,
if I'm not mistaken.

DOT:
Yes, I'm a new woman now. Before long you won't even
recognize me. Did you know the tango started in the
brothels of Buenos Aires? That's the capital city of
Argentina.

Slight Pause.

WIFF:
Who taught you to dance like that? Ned?   *DOT
crosses and shuts off the gramophone.*   I never knowed
you had it in you, maid. Why didn't you tell me you liked
to dance?

DOT:
There's a lot you don't know about me, Wiff Roach. And
a lot I don't know about you. This past month has made
me wonder if we knows each other at all.

WIFF:
Don't say that.

DOT:
It's true.

Slight Pause.

WIFF:
Why don't you ask me what *I've* been doing? Go on.

DOT:

There's only one t'ing I wants to know, and if you haven't done it, then I'm not interested.

Slight Pause.

WIFF:

Look, I talked to Dr. Hunter. He said ten out of every hundred couples can't have children. Fifty percent of the time it's the woman, t'irty-five percent it's the man.

DOT:

And fifteen it's both. So?

WIFF:

So it's not'ing to be ashamed of, he said. It's just the way life is.

DOT:

We don't know yet whose fault it is, do we? It may be you, it may be me, it may not be either one of us.

Slight Pause.

WIFF:

Well, I've been doing some serious t'inking, Dot. I made our spare room into a nursery. That's what I wanted to tell you. If we do discover the worst, we could still adopt a child.

DOT:

Adopt?

WIFF:

I wouldn't mind. I'd sooner adopt than not have one.

DOT:

I'd sooner have my own. Besides, how do we know we can't have children till we've both been tested? Tell me that, you great fool!

BILLY enters from the kitchen.

BILLY:
> Uncle Wiff!

WIFF:
> Hello, my love.　　　*He sets his fedora on his head, picks up BILLY, and ruffles his hair.*

BILLY:
> Want to see my tonsils? They're in the icebox.

DOT:
> Your Uncle Wiff was just leaving, Billy.
> *Pointedly.*　　　Wasn't you, Wiff?

> *JACOB comes down the stairs, dressed in clean slacks and an open-necked shirt.*

JACOB:
> Don't give the man the bum's rush, Dot. I invited him here.

DOT:
> You?

JACOB:
> I'm sure Jerome will be tickled pink. After all, him and Wiff served in the same regiment. How long's it been since you saw him, Wiff?

WIFF:
> The Captain? Not since the War ended.

JACOB:　　　*to DOT*
> You see? It'll be kind of like a reunion. Two old comrades in arms exchanging numbers.

WIFF:

Besides, Dot, he'd be expecting us both here. I don't see
the need for gossip, do you? . . .   *He sets BILLY
down.*   So what do you say, Billy? Let's you and
Uncle Wiff go to the kitchen and peer at the biggest set of
tonsils in the whole world.   *He and BILLY exit into the
kitchen.*

DOT: *stares at JACOB*

You don't fool me, Jacob Mercer. Not one bit.

JACOB:

What?

DOT:

What? You and Wiff cooked this up together, didn't you?
Just to get Wiff in the door?

JACOB:

Dot, I'm the first to admit he can be a pain in the arse.
But he can't be all bad, or why did you marry him?

DOT:

Don't suppose that question hasn't crossed my mind in
the past month.   *She exits upstairs.*

JACOB: *to himself*

She's some hard case, that one.   *He exits onto the
porch—to BEN.*   Ah, just the fellow I wants to see.
Your mother said not to let you sit out here too long.

BEN:

I'm not cold.

JACOB:

No, you'm like me: you don't like being cooped up . . .
        He sits beside BEN.   Listen, Ben, about that
secret of yours . . .

BEN:

What about it?

JACOB:
Grown-ups are no good, Ben, at keeping secrets. Your
mother couldn't keep it to herself.   *BEN lowers his
head.*   It's okay, my son. I prob'bly would've got
the strap myself except I never went far enough in
school . . . Did it hurt?

BEN:
Did it ever! It was like . . .

JACOB:
Like what?

BEN:
Like when I play second base and some batter belts a line
drive and I catch it with my bare hands. And how your
hands sting like crazy and you want to tuck them into
your armpits.

JACOB:
Like that, huh?

BEN:
Just like that, Dad. Seven on each hand is like fourteen
line drives from a brand-new softball, catching them with
your bare hands one after another.

JACOB:
You've got small hands, too. That makes it worse.

BEN:
I know.

Slight Pause.

JACOB:
What was you fighting about, Ben? Your mother said it
was somet'ing Junior said to you. Is that right?
BEN nods.   What was it?

BEN:

Dad, was there really a sign at Sunnyside Swimming Pool during the War? 'No dogs or Jews allowed'?

JACOB:

I heard tell there was. Why?

BEN:

'Cause that's what Junior said his father told him. 'The only mistake they made,' Junior said, 'was not adding Newfies to the list.'

JACOB:

Is that why you struck him?   *BEN nods.*
Well, Junior's just repeating what he's heard his father say. The same way the other kids call Junior a DP without knowing what it means.

BEN:

They call him a Wop, too.

JACOB:

They don't know any better. A Wop is someone without papers. A DP is a displaced person. There was at least a million people like that in Europe after the War. Poles. Estonians. Jews. People like that.

BEN:

So they came here?

JACOB:

That's right. You'd see them at Union Station, with tickets in their lapels. The Jewish kids had tickets around their necks, on a string with a lead seal.

BEN:

Which were we, Dad? DPs or Wops?

JACOB:
  Wops? Go on with you. We had British passports. We
  come from Britain's oldest colony. Four hundred and
  eighty-one years old.

BEN:
  Were we DPs then?

JACOB:
  No, we left Newfoundland in '45 of our own free will.
  And two nights from now we'll be part of a larger
  country. How do you feel about that, Ben?

JACOB:
  Okay, I guess . . .

JACOB:
  Just promise me one t'ing, my son. Don't ever let people
  like Junior make you ashamed of where you comes from.
  Promise?   *BEN nods.*   Good. Now go inside
  and give Billy back his comic book. Your mother says he
  wasn't finished with it.   *He ushers BEN inside the
  house. BEN heads for the kitchen.*   And tell your Uncle
  Wiff I wants to speak to him . . .   *BEN exits.*
  *JACOB crosses into the dining room, stopping at the sideboard.
  To himself.*   Wops! My God, that's a good one!
  Chuckling to himself, he pours two glasses of rye.

        *WIFF enters from the kitchen, turning the felt brim of his
        fedora.*

WIFF:
  You wanted to talk to me, Jake?

JACOB: *hands WIFF a drink*
  Here. And for God's sake, give me that hat.   *He
  takes WIFF's fedora and hangs it up in the hall. He returns to the
  living room and watches WIFF who is now seated on the
  chesterfield, sipping his rye.*   All right, out with it. You
  didn't just wander by tonight, did you? Who told you
  Jerome would be here?

WIFF:
Aunt Rachel.

JACOB:
That figures.

WIFF:
Captain McKenzie asked about me. And don't forget, he
mentioned me in the first dispatch he ever wrote for the
Evening Telegram: Sergeant Wiff Roach, 166th Field
Regiment. The one the Captain wrote from North Africa.

JACOB:
Stop calling him that, will you? He's not in the Army
now. Captain!

WIFF:
I'll always t'ink of him that way, Jake. Jesus, we marched
into Berlin together. He saved my life once in the desert.

JACOB:
So you told me.

WIFF:
The best damn officer I ever served under, bar none.
That's why he won the Military Cross. 'For conspicuous
bravery, coolness and outstanding conduct under fire.'

JACOB:
All right, don't get carried away, just 'cause he was
decorated once.

WIFF:
Twice.

JACOB:
What?

WIFF:

    He won two medals, Jake. The Military Cross plus the Medal of the British Empire. The Mad Captain, we called him.

JACOB:

    The Mad Captain?

WIFF:

    And my God, he was some hand with the women. Always quoting this poem or that. He'd no sooner smile than he had their pants off.

JACOB:

    No bloody wonder. Strutting about with a chestful of medals.

WIFF:

    He only wore the same ribbon we all did: the Africa Star. No, he had a quiet power all his own, the Captain. And a tongue on him as smooth as a pair of silk stockings.

JACOB:

    Well, I'm sure no merchant's son can put his heart into any piece he writes for the *Evening Telegram*. He'd never be allowed to show his true colours in a paper that supports Confederation . . . Here, let me fill that up.

    He takes WIFF's glass and his own into the dining room. At the sideboard he discovers the bottle of rye is almost empty and enters the kitchen to get another.

    During this JEROME MCKENZIE and GRACE WILCOX enter from the street, escorted by NORMAN. JEROME is forty-three, and handsome. He wears a fedora, tweed jacket with a mourning tie, and slacks. GRACE is an attractive, well-dressed English woman in her mid-thirties. She carries a camera with the flash already screwed in.

NORMAN:
>I saw you looking at the houses, I did, and I knew you must be Mary's old beau from the newspaper . . . *JEROME and GRACE exchange a look.* . . . Well, this is the house. They're all expecting you. By the way, my name's Norman Harris. Two *r*'s, one *s*.

JEROME: *looking at the house*
>You've been a big help, Norman. Thank you.

NORMAN: *to GRACE*
>What'd he say?

GRACE:
>He said he'll try and work you into the story.

NORMAN:
>Oh, that'd be nice . . . Well, just go right in. Nobody knocks. Goodbye, now. Goodbye. *He exits.*

>*JACOB returns from the kitchen with a full bottle of rye and pours two drinks at the sideboard.*

JACOB: *to himself*
>The Mad Captain!

GRACE:
>It appears the whole world knows about your romantic past, J.M.

JEROME:
>Stop it, Grace. And remember what I said. I don't want anyone embarrassed here tonight. That includes me. Understood? *JACOB starts into the living room with the drinks.*

GRACE:
>Embarrass you? Christ, I'll be the model of decorum. So don't get your balls in an uproar. *She starts for the front door.*

JACOB: *hands WIFF his drink*
    Cheers.

WIFF:
    Cheers.

        JEROME reacts to GRACE, then follows her.

JACOB:
    By the way, Wiff, do you wear that mourning tie to the
    job every day? Or did you put it on tonight to make an
    impression?   *JEROME and GRACE are now in the
    hall. They enter the living room, unnoticed, just in time to hear
    WIFF's reply.*

WIFF:
    That's not fair, duckie. I gave six good years of my life to
    the British Army. I lost a good many friends at places like
    Cassino. Men who fought and died to protect the Mother
    Country. For what? To have Britain turn around and
    adopt us out the moment our back was turned?

JEROME: *claps twice*
    Well put, Sergeant. Well put.

WIFF:
    Christ, it's the Captain!

JACOB:
    You gave me a start, Jerome. The way you clapped, I
    t'ought the devil had us.

JEROME:
    Sorry to eavesdrop like that. I didn't want to interrupt.
        Shakes hands with JACOB.   Been a long time,
    hasn't it? I wasn't sure I'd recognize you.

JACOB:

    I see you've put on a few pounds; it looks good.   *To GRACE.*   He used to be that t'in, my dear, he'd fit inside a stovepipe.   *To JEROME.*   Wait'll Mary sees you.   *Calls up the stairs.*   Mary! Quick! Come down!

    GRACE clears her throat.

JEROME:

    Sorry, Grace. Jacob, this is Grace Wilcox, our staff photographer. Grace, this is Jacob Mercer.

GRACE:

    How do you do?

JACOB:

    Pleased to meet you, Grace.   *He takes their coats and hangs them in the hall.*

JEROME: *to GRACE*

    And that S.O.B. lurking there is the one and only, Wiff Roach. How are you, Sergeant?

WIFF: *beaming*

    I'm fine, Captain. Just fine.   *He shakes hands with JEROME, then GRACE.*

GRACE:

    Sergeant.

JEROME: *clapping WIFF on the shoulder*

    Grace, this is the man I told you about. The one who convinced that New Zealand gunner that he owned the Newfoundland Railway.

WIFF:

    Convinced him? Christ, I sold it to him, Captain. The CO made me give back the forty pounds.   *They all laugh.*

JEROME:

By the way, Jacob, I want to thank you for allowing us into your home like this. It's very gracious of you.

JACOB:

Don't even mention it. An old friend's always welcome in this house.

JEROME:

I take it Aunt Rachel told you about the piece we plan to do. The sort of human interest story the Toronto papers are doing now from the outports back home. Except in this case it'll be a family from back home living in Toronto. What we'd like to get, of course, are your views on the death of a sovereign nation. How you feel about it. That sort of thing.

JACOB:

Well, hold on, now. Strictly speaking, Jerome, she's not a Dominion anymore, Newfoundland. She hasn't run her own affairs for the past sixteen years. We've been in the hands of the Commission of Government set up by Britain. Ever since we went bankrupt.

JEROME:

True. But don't forget we were supposed to get our Constitution back again as soon as the country became solvent. We were promised that.

GRACE:

Fellows, let's save the dry stuff for later. Right now, Jacob, I'd like to meet your wife. I've heard so much about her I feel as if I already know her.

JACOB:

Yes, Wiff, why don't you get the Captain and Grace a drink? I'll hurry the women along. Mary's prob'bly too nervous to come down.   *He sets down his drink and exits upstairs.*

WIFF:

We've been drinking rye, Captain, but I'm sure Jake has a bottle of good scotch in the kitchen. How 'bout you, Grace?

JEROME:

Grace already had her quota at dinner, Sergeant. More than two drinks affects her perception.

GRACE:

There's nothing wrong with my perception, old cock. Besides, this is a special occasion—in more ways than one. So make it a double, Sergeant; straight.
JEROME gives her a look.

WIFF:

A woman after my own heart.   *He exits into the kitchen.*

JEROME:

Grace, so help me . . .

GRACE:

Darling, I'll be as nice as pie. You'll see. I just need a drink.

JEROME:

She's not a threat to you. You don't need to compete.

GRACE:

I wouldn't dream of it. You think I'd compete with a seventeen-year-old? No bloody way.

JEROME:

A seventeen-year-old? What are you talking about now?

GRACE:

Don't be obtuse, J.M.

JEROME:
Then don't talk rubbish. She's a forty-one-year-old woman with a family.

GRACE:
That's not how you remember her, though, is it? Hasn't she always been exactly the same as the night she jilted you? A slender young thing frozen in time like a snapshot?

JEROME: *stares at her a moment*
I've underestimated you, Grace.

GRACE:
Oh?

JEROME:
Yes, I think the penny just dropped. I wondered why you were so keen on doing this piece. After all, it was you who sold the paper on the idea, not me.

GRACE:
You seemed keen enough. *WIFF enters from the kitchen with a bottle of scotch and pours two drinks at the sideboard.*

JEROME: *sotto voce*
Because I knew you'd always wanted to meet her. I figured that's all it was, curiosity. I forgot how cunning you can be.

GRACE:
What are you getting at?

JEROME:
You know damn well. You thought if I saw her as she is now—some dowdy, middle-aged housewife—that I might just relinquish whatever hold she's supposed to have on me. Isn't that it? *Then.* *Isn't it?*

Just then JACOB enters down the stairs.

70

JACOB:
Women take so long to get ready, it's a wonder they ever got off the *Titanic* . . . What happened to your drinks? The Sergeant go AWOL?

WIFF: *entering with the drinks*
I was scouting the terrain, duckie, for the scotch. Here you are Grace . . . Captain. *Hands each a drink.*
I ought to warn you, Captain. The kids are dying to meet the man who hunted at night with the Goums.
MARY and DOT appear on the stairs and start down.

JACOB:
The what?

JEROME:
The Goums were a tribe of Moroccans who fought alongside us in North Africa. At first they were given a bounty for every enemy ear they brought back from patrol.

JACOB:
Jesus.

JEROME:
The brass soon put a stop to it. Someone discovered they were cutting off the ears of dead French and British troops.

MARY and DOT now stand in the entrance to the living room, both looking lovely, both looking nervous.

MARY: *teasingly*
No more stories like that, Jerome McKenzie, or I'll send you back on the next plane.

JEROME: *turns and stares at MARY—beat*
Mary? Is that you?

MARY:
Why? Have I changed that much?

JEROME:
Changed? My God, you've hardly changed at all.

MARY:
Liar.

JACOB: *covering his discomfort with humour*
Don't let him sweet talk you, Mary. I'll bet he says that to all the girls. Right, Wiff? *WIFF shrugs.*

JEROME: *takes MARY's hand*
'Thou art thy mother's glass,' Mary, 'and she in thee/ Calls back the lovely April of her prime.' *He kisses her cheek.*

WIFF: *to JACOB, sotto voce*
What did I tell you? First the poem, then the pants.
JACOB glares at him.

JACOB: *quickly*
Um, I don't t'ink Jerome ever met your sister, did he, Mary? Jerome, this is Dorothy Roach, Wiff's wife.
To DOT. I'm sure Wiff's mentioned the Captain often enough.

DOT:
Oh, yes, many times.

JACOB: *to WIFF*
No mistake.

JACOB:
Hello, Dorothy.

DOT:
Call me Dot. Everyone does.

JACOB: *indicating GRACE*
And this lovely creature here is Grace Wilcox, Jerome's photographer.

DOT:
> Hello.

GRACE:
> Hi, Dot.

MARY:
> Hello, Grace.

GRACE:
> I've wanted to meet you for a long time, Mary. And to be honest, I almost wish I hadn't.

MARY:
> Oh?

GRACE:
> I mean, I knew you'd be attractive, but God, no woman's supposed to look like that after forty. How do you keep so slim?

MARY:
> There's no secret, Grace. I have two kids that run me ragged, and a husband named Jacob Mercer.

RACHEL: *enters down the stairs, dressed in a black dress*
> And if you ask me, the kids are far less trouble. But don't put that in your newspaper.

JACOB: *to WIFF, sotto voce*
> Look what she's wearing! My Christ!

JEROME:
> You're a sight for sore eyes, Aunt Rachel. Come, I want you to meet someone. Grace, this is Jacob's mother, Rachel Mercer. Aunt Rachel, this is Grace Wilcox. She'll be taking your picture tonight. *The women nod and smile.*

GRACE:
I don't think there's any question where we'll put Aunt Rachel, is there?

JEROME:
No, I want her right in the centre of the photo. We'll group the family around her. *JACOB reacts.*

GRACE:
By the way, is it possible to meet the children? What we want are three generations of the family seated around the kitchen table, Newfoundland-style. How big is the kitchen?

MARY:
I'll show you, Grace. The kids are there now. You can meet them. *MARY and GRACE exit into the kitchen.*

JACOB:
Look, let's get one t'ing straight, Jerome. Mother's not getting her picture taken in that dress. I'm surprised you'd even consider it.

RACHEL:
I buried your father in this dress; I'll wear it tonight.

JACOB:
You will like hell!

JEROME:
It's the power of the symbol, Jacob. A black dress speaks more to people back home than a thousand words.

WIFF:
True enough, Captain.

JACOB:
In that case, let her wear her wedding dress she packed away to be buried in. Wouldn't that speak more to your kind of reader?

JEROME:
It might if I worked for the *Evening Telegram*; I write for the *Daily News*, remember?

JACOB:
The *Daily News*?

JEROME:
Yes, I switched papers just before the referendum last summer. Didn't Aunt Rachel tell you?

DOT: *to RACHEL*
I knew I smelt a rat.

JACOB stares hard at RACHEL.

RACHEL:
I suppose it must've slipped my mind.   *To JEROME.*   It's not your fault, my son, it's this memory of mine.

JACOB:
Yes, the Black Widow there forgot to mention you wrote for the anti-Confederate paper. Well, there's no damn way I'll have my picture in the *Daily News*, and I won't have my kids in it, either! The rest can suit themselves!

JEROME:
Look, Jacob . . .

GRACE and MARY enter from the kitchen, trailed by BEN and BILLY. BILLY carries the Mason jar containing his tonsils.

GRACE:
The kitchen's perfect, J.M. . . . And wait'll you see what I found.   *As they all enter the living room.*
This is Ben and that's Billy. Sergeant Roach made them both honorary Goums.

MARY:
Say hello to Captain McKenzie, kids.

BEN & BILLY:
Hello, Captain McKenzie.

JEROME:
Hello, soldiers.   *Salutes.*

BILLY:
Captain McKenzie, can I have a bounty on these?
Holds up the Mason jar.

JACOB:
No, you can not. Ben, I wants you and Billy to go
upstairs. Right this minute, you hear?

BEN:
Why?

JACOB:
Don't ask questions. Just do as you'm told. Go on,
now.   *The kids exit upstairs.*

MARY:
What is it now, Jacob? What's wrong?

JEROME:
Grace and I work for the *Daily News*, Mary, not the
Evening Telegram. Aunt Rachel must've misunderstood.

JACOB:
Like hell she did!

RACHEL:
You wouldn't be speaking to me that way if your father
was alive. No mistake.

JACOB:
Go on with you. If Father was alive, you wouldn't be
wearing the dress you buried him in.

RACHEL:

> That's not funny, my son.

JEROME:

> Doesn't it bother you, Jacob, that we had Confederation rammed down our throats? Surely, it must.

JACOB:

> I don't see it that way.

JEROME:

> What about the referendum last summer? The Confederates lost on the first ballot; they only got two-fifths of the vote.

JACOB:

> The Confederates won, though, on the second ballot, didn't they?

JEROME:

> Not by much. Only eighty-five percent of the registered voters turned out. Even then the Confederates barely won by a slim margin—two percent. Or less than half of the eligible vote. And we were promised the issue would be dropped if there wasn't a clear majority.

JACOB:

> Look, Britain's been paying our bills for the last sixteen years. Maybe she just got tired of it.

RACHEL:

> And maybe Smallwood was willing to sell us out just to become the premier of the tenth province of Canada.

JACOB:

> Oh, hush up, Mother.

RACHEL:

> I won't hush up! We'd all have been better off if he'd stayed on his pig farm at Gander, him and his bow tie!

WIFF:

I couldn't agree more. Smallwood courted Canada like a bitch in heat, only it's us poor suckers who got screwed. Right, Captain?

JEROME:

Can I quote you, Sergeant?

WIFF:

Be my guest.

JACOB:

While you'm at it, why don't you ask Sergeant Roach how he'd feel if he had kids of his own? Because my two never saw fresh milk or fresh fruit till they come here. Most Newfoundlanders live in the outports, and the outports have the lowest standard of living of any place in the English-speaking world.

WIFF:

No one's denying that, duckie.

JACOB:

Why are there more of us, Wiff, living in New York City than live on the island? Why did I bring my own family here if it wasn't to find work and a better life for my kids? Tell me that!

JEROME:

I can't argue with that, Jacob. Newfoundland has always been a backward place in that sense. My concern is more with what we're losing.

JACOB:

Like what?

JEROME:

Like our sense of ourselves. The pride of an independent people. I think that's important to your kids, too.

JACOB:

It's easy to say that; you've never had an empty stomach!
It's not the rich who voted for union with Canada, you
can be damn sure! The poor just got tired of being ruled
by the iron hand of merchants like your own father!

MARY: *stepping between them*

All right, let's stop this, Jacob! Right now! I means it!

JEROME:

The ironic thing is, Mary, that my father and I voted the
same in the referendum, but for different reasons. He
wanted to keep his power and I wanted to keep our
identity. It's the sort of issue that makes for strange
bedfellows.

JACOB:

Yes, like Mother in bed with your father! Her with her
mourning dress, and him, I suppose, with his black
armband! My Christ!

MARY:

This has gone far enough, Jacob. Let's put an end to
it . . . Grace, maybe now's as good a time as any to take
that picture . . .

GRACE:

I think that's an excellent idea, don't you, J.M.?
She exits into the kitchen.

JACOB:

Suit yourselves! It just surprises me that Mary's willing to
be in that picture! She's no more against Confederation
than I am!

RACHEL:

Perhaps she's just not as pig-headed as some I could
name! Perhaps she knows it won't stop the clock, or turn
back the hands! Not for either side!   *She exits into the
kitchen.*

JACOB:
>Well, I'll be out on the porch. I needs a breath of air . . .
He starts for the front door, then stops. By the
way, Jerome, I wouldn't worry about my kids not being
proud of Newfoundland. I just had a talk with Ben
tonight on that very subject. *He exits to the porch,
slamming the door. Lights a cigarette and smokes.*

WIFF:
>He's not really sore at you, Captain. He just needs time
to cool off.

JEROME:
>I know that, Sergeant. I remember how hot-tempered his
own father was. *WIFF gestures with his glass towards
the sideboard.* No, no more for me.

DOT: *to WIFF*
>No more for you, either, till you gets your picture taken.
Go on, get in the kitchen. And take your glass with
you . . . *She winks at MARY and ushers WIFF into
the kitchen.*

>*Slight Pause.*

JEROME:
>Is it my imagination? Or did she just leave us alone?

MARY: *smiles*
>That's Dot.

>*Slight Pause.*

JEROME:
>It's good to see you again, Mary. I have to confess: I
never expected to.

>*Slight Pause.*

MARY:
>Why did you never marry?

JEROME:

Oh, I don't know. The luck of the draw, I suppose. Then again, maybe I'm not cut out for marriage.

MARY:

I don't believe that.

JEROME:

Grace does. She's the only other woman I ever asked.

MARY:

Grace?

JEROME:

Yes, we met in London during the War. She drove an ambulance for the Red Cross . . . I remember how miffed I got when she mistook me for a Canadian.

MARY:

You set her straight, did you?

JEROME:

Damn right. 'I'm no bloody Canadian,' I said. 'I'm as British as you.'

Slight Pause.

MARY:

Why did she turn you down?

JEROME:

Why? She thinks I'm carrying a torch for someone else. I suppose she respects herself too much to settle for being second best . . . Are you happy?

GRACE appears in the kitchen door.

GRACE:

J.M., we need you to decide on the grouping. You coming or not?

JEROME:
>Be right there, love.

>*GRACE hesitates, then exits.*

JEROME: *beat*
>That question was way out of line. Forgive me.
>*He stares at MARY a moment, then starts for the kitchen.*

MARY: *stopping him*
>Jerome . . . *JEROME turns, waiting.* The girl I was at seventeen is not the woman I am now. I'll never forget how confused I was the night I decided to marry Jacob. Excited but confused. I never told you that, did I?

JEROME:
>No, you didn't.

MARY:
>There was a moon on the water that night, and I sat on the steps long after Jacob had left. I expected you by any minute, remember, and part of me didn't want you ever to come. Part of me didn't want to face what I had to do . . . And then you drove up in your Touring car, and I gave you back your ring. It never did quite fit my finger . . .

JEROME:
>I still have it.

MARY:
>I saw the hurt in your face that night, and I hated myself for putting it there, and I hated you for looking that way, and Jacob for making me do that to you, and I hated life for twisting me up in knots . . .

JEROME:
>What are you saying, Mary?

MARY:

Just that a woman may wonder now and then if she's
made the right choice. Any woman, I suppose. But in her
heart she always knows. And, Jerome, I did make the
right choice. I'm sorry.

JEROME:

I understand . . .

BEN and BILLY appear on the stairs.

BEN:

Mom, can we come down now?

MARY:

No, you heard your father. Stay in your room.
JEROME exits into the kitchen.

BEN:

I thought we were getting our picture taken?

MARY:

It don't look that way. So go on, now. I'll be up later.

BILLY: *as he and BEN exit*

Aw, Jeez . . .

*MARY lingers a moment in the living room as NED
appears on the street, visibly upset.*

JACOB:

What's wrong, Ned? You'm back early, aren't you?
MARY exits into the kitchen.

NED:

Look, I didn't rush home to get my picture taken, if that's
what you're implying! So you can dispense with the snide
comments!

JACOB:

Why? What happened? Her parents didn't like your suit?

NED:

>You know what, Jacob? Sometimes you can be a real pain in the ass!   *He enters the house and exits upstairs.*

>*JACOB stamps out his cigarette, enters the house, and yells up the stairs.*

JACOB:

>You talk to me that way again, you silly bugger, and I'll take you outside and kick the shit out of you! You hear me? . . .   *He storms back to the porch, slamming the door.*   Goddamn bookworm!   *He sits on the step and stares morosely out at the street.*

>*WIFF pokes his head out of the kitchen, then comes out, followed by DOT and GRACE who pours herself a drink at the sideboard.*

DOT:

>I t'ought you said he wasn't mad at the Captain?

WIFF: *peeks out the living room window*

>I guess I was wrong.

GRACE:

>Someone should go out and talk to him, don't you think, Sergeant?

WIFF:

>Perhaps you should, Grace.

DOT:

>She means you, Wiff.

WIFF:

>Not on your life. I wouldn't send my worst enemy out there. Besides, I'm beginning to t'ink Mary is right, the best t'ing to do is just leave him alone.   *He exits into the kitchen.*

DOT: *meaning WIFF*

Believe it or not, Grace, he was a brave man in the War. Makes you wonder, don't it? *The women smile at each other, then enter the kitchen.*

At that moment APRIL ADAMS appears on the street. She is twenty, lovely, and boiling mad.

APRIL:

Excuse me. Does Ned Spencer live here?

JACOB:

Yes, my dear, he does. For the time being anyway. I'm Jacob Mercer, his landlord. And you must be April.

APRIL:

How did you know?

JACOB:

I figured you must be. I saw you across the street watching the house.

APRIL:

Well, actually, I followed him. The way he was acting tonight I thought maybe . . .

JACOB:

Maybe what? That he needed a good swift kick in the arse?

APRIL:

That, too.

JACOB:

Then you'd better stand in line.

APRIL:

I don't know what's wrong with him tonight. First he burns a hole in that good shirt I bought him; then he sits at the table and hardly says two words to my parents.

JACOB:
He can be a surly bugger.

APRIL:
Afterwards he tells me he doesn't want to see me anymore
and just walks off.

JACOB:
He didn't explain himself?

APRIL:
No. I could understand if he'd found someone else. I
thought maybe he had . . . God, right now I'm so mad I
could wring his neck!

JACOB:
And I'll bet you'm just the girl to do it. Look, why don't
we get to the bottom of this? Come inside, I'll fetch
him.   *He leads APRIL into the house. Calls up the
stairs.*   Ned, my son, come down a moment; you got
company!   *Smiling, he ushers APRIL into the living
room.*

        Slight Pause.

APRIL:
So you're from Dublin, too, are you, Mr. Mercer?

JACOB:
Dublin? Indeed I'm not. Dublin is the capital of the
Republic of Ireland.

APRIL:
Where are you from then, Northern Ireland?

JACOB:
Northern Ireland? No, I'm from Coley's P'int.

APRIL:
Where's that, if it's not in Ireland?

JACOB:
Where? It's in Conception Bay, Newfoundland, the same place as Ned comes from.

APRIL:
Ned? Ned doesn't come from there. Ned comes from Dublin.

JACOB:
Who told you that?

APRIL:
He did.

JACOB:
So Ned comes from Dublin, does he? *Calls back up the stairs.* Hurry up, Ned, I got a surprise for you! *To APRIL.* He told you that himself, did he? That he was born and raised in Ireland?

APRIL:
Yes . . .

JACOB:
Imagine that.

Just then NED comes down the stairs, dressed in more casual clothes. He stops dead when he sees APRIL.

NED:
April? What are you doing here?

JACOB:
She's recruiting for the IRA, what else.

APRIL:
I notice you've dropped your Irish accent, Ned. Now I understand why you never brought me around. You knew I'd find out what an imposter you are.

NED:

Look, I've wanted to tell you the truth for weeks now. I almost confessed tonight at the table.

APRIL:

Oh, sure.

NED:

I did. But just at that moment your mother asked me what part of Ireland I was from, remember?

APRIL:

What did you expect? You sounded like you were collecting for the Irish Benevolent Society.

NED:

Well, you could've let me answer for myself. You didn't have to tell her I came from Dublin.

APRIL:

I didn't know my father felt that way.

NED:

'Dublin?' he said. 'Wasn't Dublin neutral in the War?' And he stared at me like I was some kind of traitor. Like I'd planted a bomb in the basement.

APRIL:

It was the perfect time to tell the truth.

NED:

I thought so, too. Except right then your mother changed the subject. 'Isn't it awful,' she said, 'the expense that Newfoundland will bring on the Canadian taxpayers?' That's when I decided it wasn't such a perfect time after all.

APRIL:

No, you'd rather break up with me than admit to being a snob. Did you think I wouldn't go out with you if I knew you came from Newfoundland? Is that it?

JACOB:

Go on, Ned. Answer the girl.

NED:

Look, just butt out, Jacob!

APRIL:

You think James Joyce ever denied his race? Or Yeats?
Or any of those other writers you admire?

NED:

I don't deny what I am, damnit.

APRIL:

I think you do. I've never read your stories, Ned, but I'll
bet there's not a trace of your homeland in a single one.

NED:

Listen, I've lived in this city now for four years. And if I
choose to write about it, that's my business.

APRIL:

Keep telling yourself that, Ned. It may be why your
stories never get published . . . Anyway, I'm glad I came
here tonight; I might still be wondering what *I*'d done
wrong. Goodnight, Mr. Mercer, and thanks.   *She
starts for the hall, then turns.*   Joyce lived in Paris most
of his life, Ned. Is that where he chose to set *Ulysses*? . . .
And with that she exits.

JACOB:

What did she mean by that?

NED: *about to go upstairs*

James Joyce was an Irish writer. He wrote a book called
Ulysses that takes place in Dublin.

JACOB: *stopping him*
In other words, he wasn't ashamed of his people, is that
it? Not like you, huh, Ned?

NED:
I'm not ashamed, or why would I be living here?

JACOB:
You can't afford to live anywhere else, that's why.
You've boarded here for four years, Ned, and you've yet
to bring home a single friend. Why is that? . . .
NED says nothing.   Any man who carries that kind of
shame inside him will be crippled for life. Mark my
words.

NED:
Like Ben, I suppose?

JACOB:
Ben?

NED:
Yeah, Ben. Yesterday I was coming home from work,
and I saw that Sanilosi kid and two others kicking the shit
out of him. I broke it up.

JACOB:
Yesterday? . . .

NED:
They had him down on the street in front of Mike's Fruit
Market, trying to stuff rotten lettuce into his mouth . . .
JACOB winces   . . . And you know why,
Jacob? You know why?

JACOB:
Tell me!

NED:

Junior was sitting on his chest, screaming, 'You're just a
Newfie, Mercer! Say it! Say it!' and Ben was screaming
back, 'I'm not a Newfie! I'm not! I'm not a fucking
Newfie!'

JACOB:

Ben said that? . . .

NED:

Yeah, Ben said that. Over and over. 'I'm not a fucking
Newfie! I'm not!'

JACOB:

Then what was that fight all about in school today?
Then.   Ned?

NED:

Maybe it wasn't what you thought, Jacob. Maybe it
wasn't that Junior insulted Newfoundlanders. Maybe
Ben was just upset that Junior called him one. Did that
ever occur to you?

JACOB:

No. No, it didn't . . .

NED:

You preach to me about pride, Jacob, but what kind of
pride are you teaching him? What the hell does Ben know
about Newfoundland except that his own father can't
wait to give it away? So don't be surprised if he grows up
thinking he's second-class, and wondering why he feels
that way.   *He looks at JACOB a moment, then starts for
the stairs.*

JACOB: *springs from the chair*
Goddamnit, Ned!

NED:

    What?

JACOB:

    The kids are upstairs! Tell them both to get down here on the double! Tell them we'm all getting our picture taken! And while you'm at it, tell Ben to go into my closet and bring down that black tie of mine! Maybe you can tie the knot for me!

    Curtain.

ACT TWO

Scene I

It is the next night, Wednesday, March 30th. The porch light is on. A black flag has now replaced the Union Jack.

DOT and NORMAN are waltzing in the living room to a record that plays on the gramophone. RACHEL sits in the alcove in the dining room, listening in to the party line.

DOT:
Very good, Norman. Very good.   *NORMAN's hand slides down onto DOT's backside, and she tactfully lifts his hand onto her waist.*

RACHEL: *her hand over the mouthpiece*
Dot, you'll never credit this, but that woman who works at the bakery has a tattoo of a spider on her left hip.

DOT: *still dancing*
How do you know that?

RACHEL:

> I just heard her say so. Imagine confiding that to Walt the butcher, and him panting worse than Norman.

DOT:

> Well, you better not let Jacob catch you listening in. He t'inks it sets a bad example for the kids . . .   *The record ends, and DOT crosses to the gramophone to lift the arm.*

RACHEL:

> The kids are at the movies. Besides, at my age it's the only bad example left to set. Not to mention the only excitement clear of Norman dropping in with his Guy Lombardo records. You'd t'ink after all these years he'd give up.

NORMAN: *to DOT*
> What'd she say?

DOT:

> She said next time, Norman, she'll be sure to save you a dance!

NORMAN:

> Now wouldn't that be nice!

RACHEL:

> Don't you encourage him, Dot. And don't let him forget the time.

DOT:

> The time, Norman! The time!

NORMAN:

> Oh, yes, I have to get back now, I do.   *Collects his records.*   I don't want to burn my hot cross buns . . . Goodnight, Rachel! I wouldn't worry too much about Ned! I'm sure it's not too serious!

DOT:

> Goodnight, Norman.

NORMAN starts for the front door, just as DR. HUNTER, wearing an overcoat and fedora, enters from the street, carrying his black bag. The doctor halts, noticing the black flag, then continues up the steps to the porch where he meets NORMAN.

DR. HUNTER:
Evening, Norman.

NORMAN:
You're just in time, Doctor. Rachel's so anxious about Ned, she is, the poor woman hardly gave me the time of day. *He hurries off.*

RACHEL: *to DOT*
He's t'reatening to t'row her down on the sawdust floor of his shop the next time she comes in and peel off every stitch of her clothes. That's the last time I'll ever buy meat from that man.

During this DR. HUNTER removes his fedora, smooths down his hair, and crosses to the front door. We hear the doorbell ring.

MARY: *off—upstairs*
Answer the door, will you, Aunt Rachel? That's probably the doctor now!

RACHEL: *into the mouthpiece*
I wish you two would stop talking and just do it! The suspense is killing me! *She hangs up.*

DOT:
I'll get it, Aunt Rachel. *She crosses quickly to the front door, while RACHEL wanders into the living room.* Good evening, Doctor.

DR. HUNTER: *entering the hall*
Evening, Dot. *DOT takes his overcoat and fedora.* Evening, Rachel.

RACHEL:
>Evening, Doctor. You didn't waste much time getting here, did you? Mary's upstairs with him.

DR. HUNTER:
>Has Ned ever had an attack like this before?

RACHEL:
>Never. We t'ought at first it was his appendix, the way he hobbled in all scrunched over.

DR. HUNTER:
>It can't be that, Rachel. He had his appendix out years ago.

RACHEL:
>So he told us.

DR. HUNTER:
>Well, I suppose I'd better go see the patient . . . Oh, by the way, Dot, you look very nice tonight. In fact, you look ravishing.

DOT:
>Why, t'ank you . . .   *The doctor smiles and exits upstairs. RACHEL stares at DOT, arching one eyebrow.* What?

RACHEL:
>I never said a word.

DOT:
>You don't have to. I can read your mind like a book.

RACHEL:
>Well, I notice he never told *me* I was ravishing.

DOT:
>Don't be foolish. He was just being nice, that's all. The way Norman's nice to you.

RACHEL:

Norman? Norman's been smitten with me since his wife died. No, I suspect the doctor has more on his mind than stethoscopes. After all, he's only human like the rest of us.

During this JACOB appears on the street and enters the house. He hangs up his cap and windbreaker, revealing a black armband on his arm. At the same time MARY comes down the stairs.

JACOB:

Isn't that the doctor's hat and coat? What's he doing here?

MARY:

Ned's not well.

JACOB:

Ned?

MARY:

He staggered in not long ago, barely able to walk. Scared us half to death.

JACOB:

I t'ought it was odd he never come home for supper. Did he say where he was to?

MARY:

No, not a word.

JACOB:

Maybe he's putting on an act. Remember how he beat his head on the wall when that story came back from *The Saturday Evening Post*?   *He crosses into the dining room and pours himself a drink.*   The boys get home from the movies?

MARY:

No, not yet . . . Which reminds me, how'd it go just now? Did you speak to Mr. Sanilosi?

JACOB:
Yes, I told him to keep Junior and his friends away from Ben—or else.

RACHEL:
How'd he take it?

JACOB:
I don't know if I did much good. The man's got a real grudge against us.

RACHEL:
A grudge? What in the world for?

JACOB:
Remember what Father did the day he returned from the Great War? How he walked to the cupboard and swept all your good dishes onto the floor?

RACHEL: *to DOT*
Yes, he smashed every cup and saucer I had: it was all made in Germany.

MARY:
What's that got to do with the Sanilosis?

JACOB:
A lot. They come from a small town on the Adriatic coast. In 1943 it was wiped out by the British Eighth Army. One of the artillery units was from Newfoundland.

MARY:
Oh.

RACHEL:
No wonder he holds a grudge.

JACOB:
There's more. He has a young sister named Teresa, and one day she spied an officer munching on an apple. 'Biscuit, Johnny,' she said. 'Biscuit, Johnny.' So this

officer took Teresa into his truck and gave her one. Only she didn't discover it till two months later when it was already in the oven.

DOT:
Men.

RACHEL:
How did she know he was a Newfoundlander?

JACOB:
Because she noticed the insignia on the fender of the truck, a gold caribou head on a red background. *He sits in the armchair and picks up his newspaper.*   For all we knows it might've been the Mad Captain up to his usual mischief.

MARY:
Oh, go on with you.

JACOB:
I wouldn't put it past him. According to Wiff all he had to do was show his teeth and the women fell like bowling pins. A regular Errol Flynn.   *He turns his attention to the paper.*

        Slight Pause.

DOT:
Speaking of Jerome, Mary, you'll never guess who he puts me in mind of. Johnny Weissmuller in that movie I saw last year, *Tarzan and the Mermaids*.

JACOB: *to MARY*
What did I tell you? 'Biscuit, Johnny. Biscuit, Johnny.'

MARY:
Don't be foolish.

JACOB:

>Why the hell can't he get a woman of his own? Why is he slinking around here, ogling another man's wife?

MARY:

>Ogling?

JACOB:

>Yes, ogling. I saw the way he was watching you last night. Oh, he put up a good front, but he didn't fool me.

RACHEL:

>That's all in your mind, my son.

JACOB:

>It is like hell. And don't t'ink Grace didn't notice. It's why she drank so much . . . There's not'ing more insulting than a man who can't keep his eyes to himself.
>*He returns to the newspaper.*

>*BEN and BILLY dash on from the street and race up the porch steps. BEN is clutching an orange wig. They halt on the porch.*

BEN:

>Now remember: keep your mouth shut. I don't want us to get into trouble.

BILLY:

>Us? It wasn't *me* who stole Miss Dunn's hair.

BEN:

>In that case, you don't get part of the bounty.

BILLY:

>What bounty?

BEN:

>Don't you remember? Captain McKenzie said he was coming by again tomorrow night. He said he'd give us a dollar if we brought something back from the enemy.

BILLY:
>   Do I get half?

BEN:
>   We'll see. For now, just let me do the talking . . .
>   *They enter the house and hang up their jackets. BEN hides the wig in the closet.*

MARY:
>   That you, kids?

BEN:
>   It's us, Mom.   *They enter the living room.*

JACOB:
>   How come you'm home so early? Didn't you like the second picture?   *BILLY looks at BEN.*   Well?

BEN:
>   We wanted to hear the last of *Mr. Chameleon*, Dad. Then listen to *The Great Gildersleeve* at eight-thirty.

BILLY:
>   *The Great Gildersleeve*? I'd sooner have hot chocolate and gingersnaps.

BEN:
>   Idiot!

MARY:
>   The cocoa you can have, but you're not listening to the radio. Dot, heat up the milk, will you? I'll run their bath . . . Come on, you two, you've both got school tomorrow.

BILLY:
>   School?   *As MARY ushers the kids upstairs.*   Do I have to go to school, Mom? I don't feel good . . .

>   *Slight Pause.*

DOT:

Look, Jacob, maybe this is not the time or place, and maybe it's none of my business . . .

JACOB:

Go on. Say it.

DOT:

Well, why do you keep harping on Jerome? The more you sneers at him, the more Mary digs in her heels.

JACOB:

So I've noticed.

RACHEL:

Then why do it, if it makes her cross?

JACOB:

Why? Because I'm sick of hearing what a goddamn prize he is. Handsome, rich, ex-schoolteacher, news reporter, War hero. Christ, next he'll be running for premier.

DOT:

Still, it was you she chose twenty years ago, not him.

JACOB:

She was just a girl, Dot.

DOT:

Maybe she was, but she was woman enough to know who she wanted her kids with. And if she's ever had any regrets, she's kept them to herself.

JACOB:

Yes, she keeps a lot to herself, Mary. Always has.

RACHEL:

It's the same with everyone. A woman can sleep beside her husband all his life and not know what's really in his heart. It was that way with us, your father and me . . .

JACOB:
Oh?

RACHEL:
Dot, why don't you make that cocoa? I wants to talk to
my son alone.

DOT glances at JACOB, then exits.

JACOB: *beat*
What is it?   *Then.*   Mother?

RACHEL:
I swore I'd never tell this to a living soul, Jacob. So you
have to promise to do the same.

JACOB:
I won't breathe a word of it.

RACHEL:
Not even to Mary. Promise?

JACOB:
All right.

RACHEL: *beat*
Do you recall that locket your father wore around his
neck? The one he was wearing the day he came back from
the War?

JACOB:
I only saw it once or twice. A plain silver locket, wasn't it?

RACHEL:
Yes, and he wore it inside his shirt from the day he got it
overseas till the day he died. Did you ever wonder what
was in it?

JACOB:
I wondered, yes. He wasn't the sort of man to wear a
locket around his neck.

RACHEL:

No more than he was the sort you asked questions of . . .
At first I wanted to know what was inside, but I didn't
dare ask. I figured if he wanted me to know he'd tell me
in his own time.

JACOB:

Did he?

RACHEL:

No, not a word. And later on there was no need to ask,
because I knowed. I could scarcely sleep some nights,
knowing he was lying next to me with another woman's
picture in that locket.

JACOB: *incredulous*

Another woman? Father? . . .

RACHEL:

I even knowed the woman's name. It was Betty Driscoll,
a Red Cross nurse in England.

JACOB:

You mean to tell me he was in love with another woman,
and you knowed about it all those years?

RACHEL:

Just listen.

JACOB:

All right. But how'd you come to learn her name?

RACHEL:

That was the easy part. I went over all the letters he'd
sent me that time he was wounded at the Somme. They'd
shipped him back to England, remember, to the hospital
there . . . In the first of those letters he mentioned how
kind the nurses was, one in particular, and how she was
even writing the letter for him. That's when I saw again
the name that would prey on my mind the rest of my

married life: Betty Driscoll . . . Yes, it was all there in those letters, as plain as the nose on my face, only I'd never picked up on it before.

JACOB:
Look, you sure you wants to tell me this . . . ?

RACHEL: *going on*
There was even a part of me could understand. I wasn't fool enough to expect he'd never look at another woman, being away like that all those years. I just never expected him to carry her picture home and wear it so brazenly around his neck. That's what angered me the most. That's the part I couldn't forgive . . . And as the years went by, I'd imagine what she looked like, this Nursing Sister, this Betty Driscoll. Sometimes she'd be small and slight and soft-spoken; other times she'd be coarse. But no odds how she looked, she'd always be dressed in that starched white skirt with its sky blue blouse and black shoes . . . And with time I hardened my heart to him, little by little, out of the hurt I was feeling . . . One summer's night the smell of honeysuckle woke me, and I saw him at the open window, sitting in the blue light of the moon. I wanted so bad to cross that distance between the bed and the window, but there was too much pride in me, and the distance was too great . . . And then the cancer struck him, and he bore that, too, in the only way he could, in silence. And just before the end, he turned his face towards me, working his eyes as though he was trying to tell me somet'ing. Only now he didn't have the strength to speak, not even if he wanted to . . .

JACOB:
What do you suppose he was trying to say?

RACHEL:
Oh, I understood, all right, he was searching my face to see if I forgave him.

JACOB:
And did you? Forgive him?

RACHEL:
> No. Not even then. Not so long as he was wearing that silver locket . . .

JACOB:
> Christ!

RACHEL:
> When he died, I washed and dressed him in his Sunday suit, remember, and we waked him in the parlour.

JACOB:
> I remembers.

RACHEL:
> On the last night I went up to the bedroom and took down those letters from the top shelf of the closet. I read each one again that Betty Driscoll had scribbled in her neat little hand from that hospital room in England. And then I burnt them. I marched downstairs and flung them in the stove. Then I went to the casket and gazed down at Esau. I raised the flat of my hand to strike him . . . I didn't, though. Instead I took the locket off his neck and opened it, and in the light of the lamp I studied the face of the young woman inside . . .

JACOB:
> Was she at all the way you imagined?

RACHEL:
> Not in the least. It wasn't even a pretty face in particular. And the camera had caught her squinting into the sun, which made her look far too serious. A little grim, even . . . But I could still recall the day he'd snapped that picture, Esau, and how the wind had lifted the hem of my skirt in the road outside the house . . .

JACOB: *beat*
> It was you? . . .

RACHEL: *shaken*
Yes, it was my picture all those years. And suddenly I
realized: those letters . . . his silences . . . even the look
in his eyes at the end . . . all of it misunderstood. For
nineteen years I'd walked around with that woman's face
in amber, holding it up to the light of my own suspicions.
The only real t'ing, as it turned out, was the shame I felt
at that moment, and the remorse I've lived with ever
since . . .

Silence.

JACOB: *anguished*
Why does he show up after all these years, Mother? *Why?*

RACHEL:
It's all my fault. I never should've invited him.

*DR. HUNTER comes down the stairs, carrying his black
bag, a hint of a smile on his face.*

DR. HUNTER:
Evening, Jacob.

JACOB:
Doctor.

RACHEL:
How's young Ned, Doctor? Is he going to live?

DR. HUNTER:
Oh, I'd say so. At least now he's walking upright.
Chuckling to himself, he crosses into the hall and gets his overcoat.

JACOB and RACHEL exchange a puzzled look.

RACHEL:
Do you have to rush off, Doctor? I was going to offer you
a cup of tea.

DR. HUNTER: *returning to the living room with his coat*
Not tonight, Rachel. I have an operation in the morning.

RACHEL:
Hold on then. I'll get you that bottle of parsnip wine I
promised.   *She exits into the kitchen.*

JACOB:
Where the hell was he today, Doctor? Did he say?

DR. HUNTER:
Where? In the arms of another woman, where else?
He sets down his coat.

JACOB:
Ned?

DR. HUNTER:
Someone he met in a coffee shop. Fortunately for him it
was after work. Or unfortunately, as it turned out.

JACOB:
The way Mary told it he could barely walk in the door.

DR. HUNTER:
I'm not surprised. It's only the second case of its kind I've
come across. The first was a young medical student
named Daniel Hunter.

JACOB:
You?

DR. HUNTER:
I'm afraid so. I remember one night I took a certain girl
out in my father's old Maxwell. We parked in a field and
necked and petted. I don't have to tell you how
frustrating *that* can be. When I arrived home at dawn, I
was in such agony I couldn't climb out of the car. I kept
my hand on the horn till my father came out.

JACOB:
So in other words, you and Ned had . . .

DR. HUNTER:
Precisely. Blue balls.

JACOB:
Blue balls?

DR. HUNTER:
Commonly known as 'lover's nuts.'   *He laughs.*
Luckily, my father was a doctor himself and had a
sense of humour.

RACHEL: *returns from the kitchen with the bottle of
parsnip wine*
Here's the wine, Doctor. Sorry you can't stay for a spell.

DR. HUNTER: *putting the bottle in his bag*
Well, if no one objects, I'd like to drop in tomorrow
night. I'd be honoured to share the historic moment with
the family.

RACHEL:
You'm more than welcome, my son. But there won't be
much celebrating here.

DR. HUNTER:
Yes, I noticed the black flag on the porch. Whose idea
was that?

MARY: *entering down the stairs*
It wasn't mine, Doctor, I can tell you that. Jacob t'inks
he has to do it for the kids.

JACOB:
She don't understand.

MARY:
>No, and that I don't. I'm looking ahead to the future, not back to the past. *Calls out.* Dot, is that cocoa ready yet?

DOT: *off*
>Coming!

MARY: *calls up the stairs*
>Come on, you two Goums, before the cocoa gets cold!

>>*DOT enters from the kitchen with two mugs of hot chocolate which she sets on the dining room table. Then she continues on into the living room.*

DR. HUNTER: *putting on his coat*
>Well, I suppose I'd better be off. *To MARY.* I invited myself over tomorrow night, Mary. I hope that's not inconvenient.

MARY:
>Of course not, Doctor. *RACHEL and DOT exchange a look.*

RACHEL:
>Don't forget, my son: midnight in Newfoundland is half-past ten our time. *She exits into the kitchen.*

DOCTOR:
>I'll remember . . . Goodnight, Dot.

DOT:
>Goodnight, Doctor.

>>*JACOB walks the doctor into the hall. At the same time BEN and BILLY race down the stairs, dressed as Goums, both wear turbans, pajamas under bathrobes, and each carries a wooden rifle. They enter the dining room, set their rifles on the table, and sip their hot chocolate.*

DR. HUNTER: *to JACOB*
By the way, I convinced Ned he has to get April back. Do me a favour and make sure he doesn't miss his dance class tonight.   *Puts on his fedora.*

JACOB:
Doctor, you can count on it . . . Goodnight, now.
MARY sits and knits. DOT looks through the records.

   The doctor exits onto the porch, just as WIFF enters from the street.

WIFF:
Hello, Dan.

DR. HUNTER:
Well, hello there, Wiff. I'm glad we bumped into each other. I was intending to call you.

WIFF:
Oh?   *JACOB sits in the armchair and reads his newspaper.*

DR. HUNTER:
I had a chat with your wife yesterday. She thought I might be able to persuade you to have that test we talked about. Remember?

   WIFF nods. He sits on the steps and removes a mickey of rye from the inside pocket of his overcoat. RACHEL enters the dining room.

RACHEL: *to the kids*
Take that cocoa into the kitchen. Go on. And take those guns with you . . .   *She ushers the two kids into the kitchen and exits behind them.*

WIFF:
What if I told you I'd already been to the Clinic? That I just didn't know how to break the news?

DR. HUNTER:
You've had the test?

WIFF:
Weeks ago.

DR. HUNTER:
I see . . .

WIFF:
Christ, Dan, I've tried to tell her. I keep choking on the words . . . *Takes a long drink.*

JACOB: *looks up from his paper*
I don't t'ink Jerome looks a bit like Johnny Weissmuller. I t'ink Dot needs her eyes tested. *MARY and DOT exchange a look, then ignore him.*

DR. HUNTER:
You know, Wiff, I had a patient once who contracted mumps in his early twenties. Consequently there was no sperm at all in his semen. He refused to tell his wife for fear she'd divorce him.

WIFF:
Dot would never do that, Dan. Besides, I've never been sick a day in my life, not even in the Army . . .
Takes a folded piece of paper from his pocket and hands it to the doctor. Here's the report. Read it.

The doctor looks over the report, frowning.

DR. HUNTER:
Why the hell haven't you shown her this?

WIFF:
Dan, she wants a child more than her next breath. I'd sooner cut off my tongue than have to tell her.

DR. HUNTER:
   Tell her what? For God's sake, man, this is good news.
   Just because you're not sterile doesn't mean she is. The
   important thing now is to run some tests on her, and soon.

WIFF:
   What if it *is* her, Dan? What then?

DR. HUNTER:
   Then we'll deal with it. Meanwhile, damnit, you have a
   moral duty to show her this report.   *Hands it back.*

WIFF:
   She had TB when she was young, don't forget.

DR. HUNTER: *, angrily*
   Who the hell's the doctor here, Wiff, you or me? Now go
   on and tell her. She'll be happy to know her husband's
   fertile.   *He picks up his bag and exits.*

WIFF:
   Jesus wept!   *He stoppers the mickey and slips it back in
   his pocket. Then he rises and crosses to the front door.*

   RACHEL appears in the kitchen door.

RACHEL: *calls out*
   Billy says he's hungry, Mary! He wants a bowl of that
   chowder Norman brought over!

MARY:
   All right, but then it's bedtime. Don't listen to any more
   excuses.

   The doorbell rings.

RACHEL:
   That'll be Dr. Hunter. No doubt he forgot his hat
   again.   *She exits into the kitchen.*

DOT:
 I'll get it. *She crosses to the front door.*

JACOB:
 It's right on the tip of my tongue who he reminds me of,
 Jerome.

MARY:
 And you won't rest till you have it, will you?

DOT: *returns and takes her coat from the closet*
 It's not the doctor, it's Wiff. He wants to speak to me
 outside. *DOT starts for the front door, and WIFF
 appears again on the porch, staring up at the sky.*

MARY:
 What do you suppose he wants?

JACOB:
 Beats me.

WIFF: *as DOT joins him on the porch*
 Look, maid, there's a moon out. See?

DOT:
 So there is. *Slips on her coat.*

WIFF: *beat*
 What if we couldn't have children, Dot? What then?
 That wouldn't be the end of the world, would it? After
 all, we'd still have each other.

DOT:
 Is that all you wanted to say to me?

WIFF:
 No, I . . . Sit down a moment, maid.

DOT:
 I'd sooner stand.

WIFF:

Suit yourself . . . I always figured a man and a woman got married and sooner or later had a family. Like Jake and Mary. That's the way of the world. But for some, Dot, it's not that easy. The doctor explained it to me this way. Wiff, he said, imagine that somewhere out in the Atlantic Ocean there was a bottle bobbing around with a pearl inside. And then you sends out ten million sailors in ten million dories to try and find that bottle. Only the sailors are all blind.

DOT:

Blind?

WIFF:

Yes, and even if one poor bugger happens to bump his dory into the bottle he still couldn't get the pearl out.

DOT:

Why not?

WIFF:

Why not? Because he left his corkscrew at home in his other pants. Dot, it would take *sixty million* blind sailors, he said, all rowing around in circles just to make the odds great enough so that one man might find that bottle who remembered to bring along an opener. The miracle, duckie, is how any woman ever gets pregnant . . .

DOT:

Still, it only takes one sperm to fertilize one egg.

WIFF:

Yes, just one . . .   *He moves a few feet away.*

DOT:

There's somet'ing you're not telling me, Wiff. What is it?

WIFF:

I won't beat around the bush, Dot. I had that test done the week before you moved out. I just couldn't tell you.

DOT:

What? You've had the report a whole month and you never showed it to me? You kept me in the dark all this time? You and the doctor?

WIFF:

The doctor didn't know. I only just told him.

DOT: *angrily*

Why couldn't you tell me, Wiff? I'm your wife!

WIFF:

Why? I just couldn't bring myself to hurt you. You see, maid . . .

DOT:

What?

WIFF:

Well . . .

DOT:

Well what?

WIFF:

Well, for some reason, Dot, there's no sperm at all in my semen.

DOT:

None?

WIFF:

Not a single sailor, blind or otherwise. The only t'ing that might account for it was the fact I had the mumps in the Army.

DOT:

The mumps? Sure, you never told me you had the mumps.

WIFF:

It was long ago. It didn't seem important at the time . . .

JACOB:

I just remembered, Mary. Jerome's the spitting image of Herman Brix. He played in *Tarzan and the Green Goddess*.

MARY:

Herman, my foot.

DOT:

Let me understand, Wiff. Are you telling me not'ing can be done to help you?

WIFF:

It don't look that way, maid. Damnit, it's like a bad hand that life has dealt me.

JACOB:

It's either Herman Brix or Buster Crabbe. Buster was in *Tarzan the Fearless*, wasn't he?

DOT:

Why did you let me make a fool of myself, Wiff? Letting me move out? Letting me get my hopes up? Is that how you punishes me for the past?

WIFF:

It has not'ing to do with that. I was afraid, that's all.

DOT:

Afraid?

WIFF:

Some women would divorce their husbands for a lot less. I suppose I was ashamed, too.

DOT:

The shame I can understand. But you knows as well as I do that I'd never divorce you. *WIFF says nothing.*

All right, so you've told me. That's that. And now I'm going inside, Wiff. I've got a lot to t'ink about. Go home, now. *She starts for the front door.*

WIFF:

Don't go yet, maid . . .

DOT:

Go home, I said! There's not'ing else to talk about tonight! *Close to tears, she enters the house, hangs up her coat, then hurries up the stairs.*

WIFF hesitates, then exits.

JACOB:

They couldn't have made up. She didn't invite Wiff in.

MARY:

No. Maybe I'd better go up and talk to her. *Sets down her knitting, rises.*

JACOB:

Look, what happens betwixt a husband and wife is nobody else's business.

MARY:

Dot's my sister.

JACOB:

She's old enough to look out for herself. The trouble with you, Mary, is you'm always taking sides.

MARY:

Like when?

JACOB:

Like when? Like every time I mentions Jerome, that's when. I can't say two words against him without you pouncing on me. I wish you was that quick to defend me.

MARY:

Yes, well, if you could only hear how foolish you sounds. Herman Brix! Buster Crabbe!

JACOB:

I wasn't being insulting. Buster Crabbe happens to be a fine-looking fellow.

MARY:

It was the way you said his name.

JACOB:

I didn't christen the poor bugger that. Maybe his real name is Jerome and he changed it to Buster. *I* would.

MARY:

The trouble with you, Jacob, is you've never gotten over feeling guilty about stealing me away. Twenty-t'ree years now, and it still eats at you. You always believed somehow you cheated me.

JACOB:

That's *your* word, Mary, not mine.

MARY:

This is exactly why I dreaded Jerome ever coming here. It's why I hardly ever mentions his name.

JACOB:

Why would you have to, with Wiff around? The Captain this, the Captain that. Christ, now they've got our kids playing soldiers.

MARY:

Yes, and while we're at it, let's talk about the kids. This is their country now, Jacob, their new home, and it's a little late in the day to be draping a black flag on the porch for some place they hardly even remembers. At their age they just wants to fit in. It's not right to make them feel different.

JACOB:

It's not right to make them feel ashamed, either. Oh, they may not have come here with tags on their necks, but they'm no different than any other immigrants. You wants them to grow up like Ned? Is that it?

MARY:

No, I wants them to have what we never had, a chance in life. Isn't that why we came here? . . . Remember what I told that Immigration man who almost turned us back? 'If you sends us home on the next boat,' I said, 'I'll take the kids and leap overboard. There's no way we're going back unless it's in a pine box.'

JACOB:

You frightened the poor man half to death. He t'ought you meant it.

MARY: *fiercely*

I did mean it! The happiest day of my life was when they put us on that train at Sydney and we went past the Bras d'Or Lake in Cape Breton. Someone said it meant Arm of Gold, and just at that moment the wild rose petals began to blow back past the window. Remember? We pressed our noses to the glass and watched for miles as those pink petals blew like a storm from the rush of the train westward. Remember that? . . .   *She stares hard at JACOB, then exits upstairs.*

> *At that moment MISS DUNN, aged 50, enters from the street in a rage. She carries a purse and is wearing a hat. She strides up the steps and crosses to the front door. NORMAN appears on the street, in his dressing gown and slippers.*

The doorbell rings.

JACOB: *to himself*
Now who the hell can that be?   *He crosses into the hall.*

NORMAN: *calls out*
You wouldn't be Dr. Hunter's nurse, would you?

JACOB: *calls upstairs*
Ned, you haven't fallen asleep, have you?   *Starts for the door.*

MISS DUNN: *appears on the porch*
No, I am not Dr. Hunter's nurse! Who are you?

NORMAN:
What's that?

MISS DUNN:
Get back to bed or I'll call the police!   *She strikes him with her purse.*

JACOB: *appears on the porch*
What can I do for you?

NORMAN:
She's from the Police Department.

MISS DUNN:
The man's a lunatic. I'm Amelia Dunn, Ben's teacher. I take it you're his father.

JACOB:
That's right.

MISS DUNN:
Then I'd like a word with your wife if she's home. And I'd like to see your son as well.   *Indicates she'd like to come in.*   Well, may I?

JACOB:

Oh, by all means . . .　　　*He lets MISS DUNN sweep past him, then turns to NORMAN.*　　　T'anks for keeping an eye on the house, Norman! You can go home now!
He follows MISS DUNN into the house.

NORMAN scurries off.

JACOB:

I'll give his mother a shout.　　*Calls upstairs.*
Mary! Come down a moment!　　*Then.*　　Ben, your teacher's here! She wishes to speak to you!　　*He follows MISS DUNN into the living room.*　　Can I take your hat and coat, Miss Dunn?　　*BEN and BILLY step out of the kitchen and stand listening.*

MISS DUNN:　　*testily*

No, you may not take my hat. This is not a social visit, I assure you. Your son stole something from me tonight at the Radio City, and I want it back.　　*BEN and BILLY look at one another, then crawl under the dining room table.*

JACOB:

Stole somet'ing? . . .

MISS DUNN:

Which just proves what I've said all along: parents are the last to know what hooligans their kids are. Maybe now your wife will believe me.

MARY:　　*enters down the stairs*
Believe you about what, Miss Dunn?

MISS DUNN:

I told you, Mrs. Mercer, what a nasty streak your son had, and you called me a liar. Maybe now you'll apologize.

JACOB: *quickly*
Miss Dunn says Ben took somet'ing from her tonight at the picture show.

MARY:
I don't believe it. Where is he? Ben!   *She enters the dining room.*   Aunt Rachel, send the kids in here!

RACHEL: *enters wiping her hands on a dish towel*
The kids? The kids are not in the kitchen. The last time I saw them they was . . .   *She lifts the corner of the tablecloth and peers under the table.*   Get out from there, you two! Scat!

> *The kids come scurrying out. BILLY darts behind RACHEL for protection.*

MARY:
Ben, did you steal somet'ing from Miss Dunn tonight? Tell me.

BEN:
No. It was an accident, Mom.

MISS DUNN: *to JACOB*
That was no accident!

MARY:
What was it you took?

> *BEN whispers it to MARY.*

MARY:
Oh, my God.

JACOB: *to MISS DUNN*
What did he say?

BEN:
But I didn't do it on purpose, Mom. I swear.

MARY:

Never mind. Go inside and tell Miss Dunn what you did with it. My God, what next.   *She ushers BEN into the living room. To BEN.*   All right, don't be afraid. Just tell us what happened.

BEN:

There's nothing to tell, Mom. We were sitting in our seats, watching *Two Guys From Texas*, and Miss Dunn came in and sat in front of us. She took off her hat and put it on the seat next to her.

JACOB:

You stole her hat?

MISS DUNN:

No, he did not steal my hat! I still have my hat on my head, don't I?

BEN:

At the end of the movie I wanted to get a Vernor's gingerale, only I guess when I stood up, the button on the sleeve of my jacket got caught in her hair.

MISS DUNN:

That's a lie! He tore it off my head in the dark and ran!

JACOB:

He ran off with your hair?

BEN:

I didn't mean to, Dad. I never knew anything was wrong till she started to chase us up the aisle. *That's* when I ran.

MISS DUNN:

If that's the case, why didn't you give it back? Why did you run from the theatre?

JACOB:

I dare say, Miss Dunn, you frightened the wits out of them.

BEN:
She did, Dad. We ran a whole block before I noticed the wig on my sleeve. Then I was too scared to go back.

MISS DUNN: *sarcastically*
What did you intend to do, bring it into class tomorrow?

BILLY:
We were saving it for Captain McKenzie. Weren't we, Ben?

MISS DUNN:
Who?

BEN: *to BILLY*
Idiot!

MARY: *quickly*
All right, Ben, what did you do with it? Miss Dunn needs her hair back.

BEN:
It's in the closet.

JACOB:
The closet? . . .

MISS DUNN: *as BEN fetches the wig*
I'll say one thing for him: he shows more imagination at home than he does in the class.   *BEN returns and hands the wig to MISS DUNN who snatches it from him.*

MARY:
What do you say, Ben?

BEN:
Sorry, Miss Dunn.

MISS DUNN:
Sorry? Well, we'll just see how sorry you are in school tomorrow.   *Starts to go.*

MARY:
> I warned you, Miss Dunn. If you ever touches my son
> again . . .

RACHEL: *cutting in*
> Oh, I wouldn't fret about that, Mary. Miss Dunn's too
> upset just now to t'ink straight.

MISS DUNN:
> Exactly what does that mean?

RACHEL: *advancing into the room*
> I'm Rachel Mercer, by the way—Ben's grandmother . . .
> From the look of you, Miss Dunn, I'd say you was
> nobody's fool. How long you been teaching, maid?

MISS DUNN:
> Twenty-seven years. Why?

RACHEL:
> Then I don't need to tell you how cruel children can be.
> All it takes is one word, and before you knows it, the
> whole school is snickering behind some poor teacher's
> back. Some stories can haunt a body for years.

MISS DUNN: *the implication sinking in*
> Oh, my God . . .

RACHEL:
> That's why I wants to nip this in the bud. I don't want
> these two charging off to school tomorrow, bragging
> about what happened in the dark of a picture show. You
> agree?

MISS DUNN:
> Yes, of course I agree. Yes.

RACHEL:
> It wouldn't be wise to use that strap again. That would
> only provoke the child. And we don't want him
> provoked, do we, Miss Dunn?

MISS DUNN:
> No. No, we certainly do not.   *Sits.*

RACHEL:
> The trouble is some children can't keep a secret to save
> themselves.

BEN:
> I can, Granny.

BILLY:
> Me, too.

RACHEL:
> All right, not a word of this to anyone, you hear? Not
> ever. Promise?

BILLY:
> Cross my heart, Granny.

JACOB:
> Ben?

BEN: *reluctantly*
> I promise.

RACHEL:
> Good. Now go on and finish your soup . . .   *The*
> *kids dash off, snickering.*   . . . Well, there you have it,
> Miss Dunn. No one but us will ever know.

MISS DUNN: *to RACHEL*
> Thank you . . . I suppose I ought to be grateful that none
> of the other teachers showed up tonight. I've seen Mr.
> Babcock there in the past. Usually on a Wednesday.

JACOB:
> Gerald wouldn't be there tonight. There's a Stanley Cup
> game on. He'd be home listening to it.

MISS DUNN:

I wondered why he wasn't there. That explains it. Are you friends of Mr. Babcock?

RACHEL:

Gerald and me came up from Newfoundland the same day. He carried my bags to the Bay Roberts station.

MISS DUNN:

Yes, he's a nice man. I was a bit disappointed he wasn't there tonight. It's always more enjoyable sharing a movie with someone.   *She rises, clutching her purse and wig.*
So.

RACHEL: *quickly*

Do you have to run off, Miss Dunn? Perhaps you'd like a cup of tea?

MISS DUNN:

A cup of tea?   *She glances at MARY.*   Oh, no, I couldn't . . .

JACOB:

Maybe Miss Dunn would like somet'ing a bit stronger.

MARY:

Jacob.

MISS DUNN:

Actually, I do take the occasional drink with my meals. Only tonight I was too nervous to eat for some reason. I don't think it's wise to drink on an empty stomach.

RACHEL:

In that case, maid, I'll warm you up a lovely bowl of chowder; then you can have a whiskey.   *MISS DUNN is about to protest.*   And I won't take no for an answer. So why don't you take off your hat and coat? On second t'ought, let me take your coat.   *She does.*

There. Now why don't you go upstairs and straighten up? Mary will show you where the bathroom's to, won't you, Mary?

MARY:
    It's this way, Miss Dunn.

MISS DUNN: *to RACHEL*
    Thank you again, Mrs. Mercer. This is all so unexpected, I must say.

RACHEL:
    Call me Aunt Rachel. Everyone does.

MISS DUNN:
    Aunt Rachel it is . . .   *And they exit.*

        RACHEL stares at JACOB.

RACHEL:
    Well?

JACOB: *calls out*
    Ben! Get in here!

RACHEL:
    Just because she strapped him don't mean he can lug home her hair like a trophy.

        BEN enters.

RACHEL:
    You robbed that woman of her dignity tonight. Do you realize that?

BEN:
    I hate her!

RACHEL:

Never mind that. Some day you'll understand what a cruel t'ing you did. A lot worse than what she did to you yesterday.

BEN:

It wasn't *you* she strapped, Granny.

RACHEL:

Don't talk back to me. Now I wants you to go in that kitchen and warm up the soup. And when it's done, I wants you to bring her in a bowl. Go on!   *BEN starts for the kitchen. RACHEL follows him into the dining room.*
    And tell your brother to bring in his soup, he can keep Miss Dunn company!   *BEN exits. RACHEL snatches up the phone.*   And as for you two . . . !
Listens. Then slams down the receiver.   Wouldn't you know it? Just when I wants to give someone a piece of my mind, there's no one there!   *She exits into the kitchen.*

BILLY enters the dining room, carrying his bowl and sits at the table. At the same time NED comes down the stairs, tucking a notebook into the inside pocket of his sportsjacket.

NED:

Well, I'm off. See you later.

JACOB:

That took you long enough.   *RACHEL enters the dining room with a cloth napkin and cutlery. She takes a cup and saucer from the sideboard and sets a place for MISS DUNN.*

NED:

I want to show April this new story I wrote today. I was trying to finish it.

JACOB:

It better not take place in Toronto.

NED:

It doesn't. It's set in Bay Roberts just after the War. A conductor on the Newfoundland Railway comes home from overseas to find his wife's run off with an officer from the American base at Argentia.

JACOB:

Oh?

RACHEL: *from the archway*

Your poor father's going to love that one.

NED:

I don't give a damn if he does or not, Mrs. Mercer.

RACHEL:

No, I suppose not.

NED:

Besides, it's not really about him. It's about the son who was living with his aunt at the time.

RACHEL:

Do you understand, Ned, why he wouldn't take you back?

NED:

Sure. I reminded him so much of me mother he couldn't stand to look at me.

RACHEL:

A man like that, Ned, is more to be pitied.

NED: *quickly*

I'm sorry. I'm late for class. Goodnight . . .
He exits to the porch, upset, and sits on the step.

JACOB:

That's the first time he's mentioned his mother in years. *Sits, reads his paper.*

NED:

Goddamnit!

RACHEL:

Still, it's harder for Ned to forgive his father. Maybe that story of his will help. *She exits into the kitchen.*

Just then APRIL appears on the street, carrying a book.

APRIL:

Ned? Is something wrong?

NED:

What are you doing here, April?

APRIL:

I was just bringing back your copy of *Dubliners*. I took it to class, but you weren't there.

NED:

Class isn't over yet.

APRIL:

I left early. I wasn't feeling well. I thought I'd drop it off on my way home. *Hands him the book.* I guess I won't be reading it now. *Beat.* Well, goodbye.

NED:

Goodbye.

APRIL:

Is that all you can say? Ned Spencer, you're an idiot. You don't know the first thing about women.

NED:

Look, *you*'re the one who broke up with *me*, remember? I'm not apologizing.

APRIL:

I suppose you think *I* should?

NED:

Do what you want. Last night you called me a liar, a snob, and a fraud; now you say I'm an idiot. I hate to say it, but you have rotten taste in men.

APRIL:

There's no need to rub it in.

NED:

What puzzles me is why you want to get back with me.

APRIL:

Who says I want to get back with you?

NED:

Then what are you doing here?

APRIL:

I already told you, I'm returning your book, you arrogant, conceited moron! *She sits on the steps and cries quietly. NED turns away, confused, not knowing what to say. RACHEL enters the dining room with a plate of biscuits which she sets on the table. MISS DUNN comes down the stairs, wearing her orange wig and carrying her purse and hat.*

JACOB:

Feel better, Miss Dunn?

MISS DUNN:

Oh, yes, thank you.

RACHEL: *enters the living room*

Go right in, Miss Dunn. I'll hang up your hat.   *She does. As MISS DUNN enters the dining room, BEN comes in from the kitchen with a bowl of chowder that he sets on the table.*

NED:

You didn't have to return the book, you know, I gave it to you.

133

APRIL:
Oh, shut up! Just leave me alone!

MISS DUNN: *meaning the soup*
Oh, doesn't that look delicious. Thank you, Benjamin.

RACHEL: *returns to the dining room*
What do you say, Ben?

BEN:
You're welcome, Miss Dunn.   *He runs into the living room and up the stairs. MISS DUNN sits at the table and samples the chowder.*

MISS DUNN:
Mmmm.

RACHEL:
I'll just put the tea on.   *She exits into the kitchen. MISS DUNN smiles at BILLY.*

NED: *to APRIL*
Look, there was *some* truth in what I told you. My great-great-great-grandfather was born in Ireland. He went to Newfoundland during the Potato Famine.

APRIL:
Really?

NED:
Not that he ever got there. He died and was buried at sea.

APRIL:
Still, he *was* Irish . . .   *She turns and looks at him.*
I was too critical of you last night, wasn't I? Look at Hemingway. He doesn't always write about Americans.

NED: *takes out his notebook and hands it to her*
Take this home and read it. It's a story I wrote today. I'm dedicating it to you.

APRIL:
You are?

NED:
It's set in Conception Bay. It's about how a young boy comes to be ashamed of his father. How he wants him to be like the American who stole his mother. Maybe it'll help you understand me.

APRIL: *tucks the notebook into her purse*
Oh, Ned, don't let's fight like that again. Let's just be honest with each other.

NED: *turns away*
How honest?

APRIL:
What do you mean?

NED:
For example, what if I'd been with another woman today? What then?

APRIL:
Ned, you don't have to try to make me jealous. I know you love me.

NED:
I do, April. *He kisses her. Suddenly he breaks the kiss and walks away.*

APRIL:
What's wrong? *Then.* Ned?

NED:
Well, I went to the coffee shop at Union Station after work. You know, to write. I like to write in crowded places. It helps me concentrate.

APRIL:
So?

NED:

So I met this woman there. She invited me back to her place.

APRIL:

So?

NED:

Why do you keep saying 'So'? Nothing happened. Honest.

APRIL:

Something did. I can tell.

NED:

We danced. Big deal.

APRIL:

How close?

NED:

What does that matter?

APRIL:

Did you kiss her?

NED:

No. Yes.

APRIL:

And you say nothing happened?

NED:

Not what you think. She was just a tease.

APRIL:

What if she hadn't been? What would you have done? Walked away?

NED:

Look, I thought we were supposed to be honest with each other?

APRIL:

I suppose you let her read your story, too?

NED:

What's wrong with that?

APRIL:

What's wrong with that is I haven't read it yet, you jerk! God, this just proves what a shallow person you really are, Ned Spencer! *Starts to go, turns.* And just because you suddenly confess doesn't mean I automatically forgive you! *And she exits.*

NED: *to the sky, quoting* Othello

'O monstrous world! Take note, take note, O world! To be direct and honest is not safe.' *He sits on the steps and stares out front.*

BILLY: *as RACHEL enters with the teapot*

Granny, I'm finished. Can I be excused?

RACHEL:

All right, but put your bowl in the sink. *BILLY exits. RACHEL pours the tea.* How's the chowder, Miss Dunn? Our neighbour next door made it.

MISS DUNN:

Oh, it's excellent, Aunt Rachel. So many delicious things in it. I especially like the snails.

RACHEL:

Snails? What snails?

BILLY bursts out of the kitchen, brandishing the empty Mason jar.

BILLY:
Look, Granny! Ben stole my tonsils! See!

RACHEL:
Don't be foolish. Why would he want to steal your . . . ?
She turns and stares at MISS DUNN. JACOB reacts.
RACHEL's eyes are riveted on MISS DUNN as she continues to
spoon the chowder. BILLY follows his grandmother's gaze and
stands transfixed.

Blackout.

Scene II

The next night, Thursday, March 31st, around 9:50. In the living room BEN and BILLY, both dressed in pajamas, are stretched out on the floor, playing Snakes & Ladders.

JACOB and WIFF are playing cards at the dining room table on which rest a bottle of whiskey and two glasses. Or more precisely, they were playing cards until WIFF got excited about the story he was telling. At the moment JACOB is seated, cards in hand, watching WIFF who is on his feet, gesticulating.

WIFF:
Anyway, that's when we saw the flash ahead of us in the dark. The man on p'int—Cobb was his name—had stepped on a mine. The Germans had retreated, booby-trapping the field.

JACOB:
   Sit down, will you?

WIFF:
   We worked our way across the ground, inch by inch, the
   Captain with the mine detector, and me tight on his
   heels, the night so black and wet we tripped over Cobb in
   the dark. Both his feet had been blown off, and one arm.

JACOB:
   Do you want to play cards or don't you?

WIFF:
   I hefted Cobb on my shoulders, Jake, and the Captain led
   the way again back across the field in the rain. For that,
   the brass awarded him the M.B.E. and the men named
   him the Mad Captain.   *He sits and picks up his cards.*
   RACHEL enters down the stairs, carrying her knitting. She turns
   on the floorlamp, sits in the armchair, and begins to knit.

JACOB: *to WIFF*
   Just don't go dredging that up once Jerome gets here.
   He's prob'bly had a bellyful of hearing how brave he is.
   Plays a card.

BEN:
   What did Dad do in the War, Granny?   *JACOB*
   reacts.

RACHEL:
   I'm not speaking to you, I'm still cross.

BILLY:
   Did he ever win a medal like Captain McKenzie?

BEN:
   Captain McKenzie won *two* medals, stupid.

JACOB: *to WIFF*
   See what you've stirred up?

140

RACHEL:
No, Billy, your father was with the Coast Defence
Battery, protecting Conception Bay from German
U-boats. No one got decorated for that.

BEN: *beat*
Grampa won a medal, didn't he, Granny? In World War
I. Didn't he?

RACHEL:
Yes, he did. Now don't bother me.

BEN:
Which was it, Granny? The Military Cross?

RACHEL:
No, he won the Military Medal, serving with the
Newfoundland Regiment at Gallipoli. He was some
proud of that, Esau.

WIFF:
He would've been proud, too, of the Captain, Aunt
Rachel. As one soldier to another.

JACOB:
Look, are you going to study those cards all night?

WIFF: *plays a card*
I'll never forget the time we celebrated St. Patrick's Day
at Cassino. That's a town in Italy, Ben . . . Sergeant
Chick Gallagher sang'Killarney'and then we all j'ined in,
all the officers and men. The best of all was when the
Captain stood up and sang'The Rose of Tralee.' You
could've heard a pin drop.

JACOB:
Christ, is there not'ing than man can't do?

WIFF: *sings*
'She was lovely and fair as the rose of the summer
Yet 'twas not her beauty alone that won me
Oh, no, 'twas the truth in her eyes ever dawning
That made me love Mary, the Rose of Tralee.'

JACOB slams down his cards.

BEN:
Granny, can we put the radio on?

JACOB: *jumps up and enters the living room*
No, you can not. Now take your Snakes & Ladders and
play upstairs. Go on. You can listen to the radio at
ten-t'irty along with the rest of us.

BEN:
We weren't doing anything.

JACOB:
Go on, I said. And change out of those pajamas. You
don't want to be dressed like that in front of company.
The kids start for the stairs.

RACHEL:
If it was up to me, Ben wouldn't be allowed out of his
room. Not after what he did to Miss Dunn last night.

BILLY: *calls back*
He thinks it's funny, too, Granny.

BEN: *to BILLY*
I do not!   *As the kids exit, DR. HUNTER appears on
the street, carrying a bottle of champagne in a paper bag.*

RACHEL: *to JACOB*
I don't suppose you've punished him yet, have you?

142

JACOB:
What can I do, Mother? I've always taught him to use his
brain instead of his brawn. A slap on the backside now
would only confuse him.

RACHEL:
No wonder he's the way he is.

> DR. HUNTER *enters the house and hangs up his overcoat
> and fedora.*

DR. HUNTER:
Evening, all!

JACOB:
Oh, hello, Doctor. Come in.

WIFF:
Evening, Dan. We took bets tonight on whether you'd
make it.

DR. HUNTER: *enters the living room, leaving the
champagne in the hall*
Make it? Wiff, I wouldn't miss this for the world.
Then. Evening, Rachel.

RACHEL:
Evening, Doctor.

DR. HUNTER:
I would've been here sooner, but I had to drive down to
the Post Office. The traffic's tied up all around Union
Station. *WIFF pours two drinks at the sideboard.*

JACOB:
Yes, there's a banquet tonight at the Royal York. The
Newfoundland Association invited eight hundred people.
They expects eight hundred more on the sidewalk.

DR. HUNTER: *sits on the chesterfield*
I wondered what was going on. I saw the Premier drive up, and the Mayor.

DOT: *off*
Wiff, I needs you to bring down my heavy suitcase!

WIFF:
Be right up, duckie! *He enters the living room and hands the doctor a drink.*

DR. HUNTER:
So, Wiff, you persuaded Dot to go home, did you? Maybe it's a good thing you showed her that report.

RACHEL:
Well, he kept his end of the bargain, Doctor, and now she's keeping hers.

WIFF:
That's right. She promised if I had the test done she'd come back, no odds how it turned out. And Dot's as good as her word. *Sets down his glass.*

DR. HUNTER:
Have her give me a call tomorrow, would you? I think it's time she saw a specialist.

WIFF:
A specialist?

RACHEL:
So it was good news after all.

DR. HUNTER:
On second thought, I'll discuss it with her later. I made an appointment today for her to see an old colleague of mine. He's the top man in his field.

WIFF:
Look, Dan, I'm not so sure . . .

DOT: *off*
　　Wiff!

JACOB:
　　I t'ink Dot means business, Wiff. I'd hurry before she
　　changes her mind.

WIFF: *to DOT*
　　All right, I'm coming!   *He looks at the doctor a moment,*
　　then exits upstairs.

DR. HUNTER:
　　Oh, I clean forgot, Rachel. I brought you something.
　　He sets down his drink, crosses into the hall, and returns with
　　the bottle of champagne.   A bottle of bubbly for tonight.

RACHEL:
　　I don't know what there is to celebrate tonight, Doctor,
　　clear of Dot's future.

DR. HUNTER:
　　Well, I was at an Irish wake once: they toasted the corpse.
　　I don't see why we can't do the same.

RACHEL:
　　I'll put the wine in the icebox for now.   *She exits into*
　　the kitchen just as WIFF comes hurrying down the stairs, lugging
　　a large suitcase which he carries out to the porch.

WIFF: *to the sky*
　　Please God, don't do this! Don't let her know I lied!

JACOB:
　　What the hell's got into Wiff? Dot must've put a match to
　　his backside.   *DOT and MARY hurry down the stairs,*
　　DOT carrying her purse.   What's the big rush, Dot?
　　What happened?

DOT:

Oh, Wiff just remembered he left the oven on at home. It'd be just like him to burn down the house. *WIFF returns to the hall, slipping on his overcoat and fedora.*

MARY:

You're sure, Wiff, you left the oven on after you took out your steak? You're positive?

WIFF:

Why would I lie about a t'ing like that? Sure I'm sure. God, I'm getting worse than Dan. *He brings in DOT's coat and helps her on with it.* Look, Mary, tell the Captain I'm sorry we missed him. He'll understand, I'm sure. *To DOT.* All set, duckie?

DOT:

What about my other suitcase?

WIFF:

Let's not worry about it now, let's go. I'll pick it up tomorrow.

DR. HUNTER:

How do you plan to get home, Wiff, with that heavy suitcase?

WIFF:

How? We'll catch a cab.

JACOB:

What? At this hour?

MARY:

I'd better call you one.

DR. HUNTER:

No, Mary, I'll drive them. I'm parked just three doors down.

146

WIFF:
Oh, I couldn't let you do that, Dan. No, no, I wouldn't hear of it.

DOT:
It'd be a lot faster to let the doctor drive us. We'd be home in no time.

DR. HUNTER:
I insist, Wiff.

MARY:
Besides, it just occurred to me: why in the world are you both rushing off? Why can't Dot stay here till you gets back?

WIFF:
Why? What do you mean, why?

DOT:
Well, there's no need of both us going, is there? The doctor can have you there and back in twenty minutes. That way we can all get to say goodbye to the Captain.

WIFF: *exploding*
For Christ's sake, I'd like to be alone with my wife, if no one minds! I've barely seen her in four weeks! The hell with the Captain! Now let's go, Dot, before the goddamn cat is asphyxiated!

RACHEL: *returns*
What's all the commotion? . . . Why have you got your coats on? Don't tell me you'm leaving, Dot?

DOT:
I'm afraid so, Aunt Rachel.

MARY:
Wiff just remembered he left the oven on.

WIFF:
   That's right. And if we don't get a move on, we may not
   have a roof over our heads.

RACHEL: *to DOT*
   It's a shame you won't be here, maid. The doctor
   brought you some good news. I was hoping to make a
   toast.

DOT:
   Good news? What good news?

WIFF: *desperate*
   Never mind now, Dot. I'll explain on the way home.
   Let's go.

DR. HUNTER:
   Anyway, I wouldn't exactly call it good news. It's just
   that I made an appointment for you to see a gynecologist,
   now that we're over the first hurdle.

DOT:
   The first hurdle? I don't understand.

WIFF: *really desperate now*
   Look, our house could be in flames this very second!
   Can't we discuss this later? Just between the two of us?

DOT:
   Hold your horses! . . .   *To DR. HUNTER.*
   Doctor, you wouldn't be sending me to a specialist,
   would you, unless Wiff's test was positive? Isn't that so?

DR. HUNTER:
   That's correct, yes. But as you know, Dot, Wiff's as
   fertile as a bull.

JACOB: *to MARY*
   He is? I t'ought you said . . . ?

WIFF: *cutting in*
Let the house burn down then, and the cat with it! I don't
give a good goddamn!

DOT:
You've read the report, Doctor? Actually read it yourself,
have you?

DR. HUNTER:
Yes, last night. That's what I meant by the first hurdle. I
thought you understood that.

DOT:
No, the bull told me he was past his prime. In fact, he told
me he had no sperm count at all.

DR. HUNTER:
No sperm count?

DOT:
Yes, he said he caught the mumps in the Army. That's
what killed all the blind sailors.

JACOB:
The blind sailors? . . .

DR. HUNTER:
Damn you, Wiff, I thought we agreed you'd show her
that report?

WIFF:
That was your idea, Dan, not mine. I'd sooner not have
kids at all than for Dot to be blaming herself.   *To
DOT.*   That's why I lied to you, maid, I swear! As
God is my witness!

JACOB: *to MARY*
What did he mean, the blind sailors?

MARY:
Not now, Jacob. Please.

WIFF: *to DOT, angrily*
And I didn't forget to turn off the goddamn oven! I never turned it on in the first place! I cooked a steak in the frying pan!

DOT:
Take it easy, Wiff. It's all right.

WIFF: *going on*
Why couldn't you just leave well enough alone? Oh, no, you wouldn't listen, would you? No, you had to keep on and keep on till you found out!

DOT:
No odds. I've always suspected it was me. *To MARY.* Remember that dream I had, Mary? It happened again last night. Do you realize now what it was trying to tell me?

MARY:
Dot, that was just a dream.

DR. HUNTER:
For God's sake, even if there is a problem, that doesn't mean something can't be done. We won't know that till you've seen Dr. Fischer.

DOT:
Oh, I'm sure he's a good man, Doctor. I'm sure he'll do all he possibly can. But there are some t'ings that just can't be fixed . . . And now if you'll all excuse me, I t'ink I'd like to be by myself . . . *She turns to go, but is stopped by WIFF's line.*

WIFF: *turned away*
I wish my test had been negative, Dot. I don't know what else to say.

DOT nods. Then she turns and looks at WIFF, and there is a small, wry smile on her lips. WIFF is still unable to look at her. (NOTE: DOT's speech is not really meant

for the others in the room, even though she often refers to
WIFF in the third person. The focus should be on WIFF,
though some of the lines might be spoken out front.)

DOT: *beat*
I'll never forget the day my husband returned from the
War. It was July 30, 1945. Remember that, Wiff? The
day the first draft of the Newfoundland Regiment sailed
home.

WIFF:
How could I forget? We hadn't seen each other in six
years.

DOT:
I stood on Signal Hill in the rain and watched the *Lady
Rodney* slip t'rough the Narrows into St. John's harbour.
It poured so hard they had to cancel the parade. I felt bad
about that for all the men, but especially for Wiff. I saw
him at the official reception at the big Furness-Withy
shed, and the next day he paraded at Shamrock Field. A
week later he was back in civilian life.

WIFF:
That's a day I won't forget, either.

DOT:
No, that was the day he packed away his uniform. Then
he went out and sat on the porch and whittled a stick. He
was there till long after dark, and he had this . . . this lost
look on his face as though he wondered what he was going
to do now with the rest of his life.   *She turns and looks
at WIFF, and there is only pity in her now for the both of them.*
I never understood, Wiff, how you felt at the time.
No, I don't suppose I understood that till just now . . .
She turns, stifling a sob, and hurries up the stairs.

Silence.

151

RACHEL: *finally*
Someone ought to go up and comfort her. And I don't
t'ink it should be Wiff.

MARY:
No, I'll go.   *RACHEL exits into the kitchen.*

DR. HUNTER:
Let me, Mary. Maybe I can undo some of the damage
Wiff's done. Right now that woman needs to be
reassured.

WIFF:
Right now, Dan, she needs a priest more than a doctor.
But don't take my word for it.

DR. HUNTER:
No, and I don't intend to.   *He looks sternly at WIFF,*
then exits upstairs.

        Slight Pause.

MARY: *to WIFF*
What did you mean before, you didn't want Dot blaming
herself? Why should she blame herself?

WIFF:
I only meant, if she found out she couldn't conceive.
That's all.

MARY:
Why should that be the outcome of the test? What makes
you so sure?

JACOB:
He didn't say he was sure, did he?

MARY:
Then why is he behaving as if he is? Any woman deserves
the chance to have a child. What right does he have to
deny her that?

WIFF:

Maybe she's already had that chance, Mary. Maybe one chance is all she's meant to have . . .

MARY:

What's that supposed to mean? That Dot had a miscarriage once? Is that why she has those dreams?

WIFF:

Don't put words in my mouth. It's just there are t'ings about Dot that even you don't know.

MARY:

Like what?

WIFF:

That's not for me to say, Mary.

MARY:

Then don't tell me I don't know my own sister. I knows her as well as I knows my husband. We've always been close, Dot and me.

WIFF:

It wasn't that way during the War, was it? Not when she lived in St. John's. You scarcely saw her then.

MARY:

What are you saying, Wiff?

WIFF:

Just that you don't know all the facts, Mary. So don't be so quick to judge.

MARY:

What facts? She worked in the kitchen of the Newfoundland Hotel. She lived in a boarding house. She wrote letters to you. She went to the movies. Those are the *facts*.

WIFF:

Yes, and she helped out at the Red Triangle Club twice a week, serving meals to visiting servicemen. That's a fact you forgot. It's also a fact a man can get lonely far from home. The same way a woman can, waiting for six long years.

MARY:

Dot was never unfaithful to you, and don't you even hint at it. Not Dot.

WIFF:

Why not? 'Cause she happens to be your sister?

MARY:

She would've told me, that's why. Dot and me have no secrets from each other. None.

WIFF:

Maybe it's somet'ing she'd sooner forget. There are some facts, Mary, not even sisters can share . . .
MARY says nothing. WIFF looks away. I could tell she was different at the Furness-Withy shed. She didn't have to tell me she'd been with someone; I knowed that. I could always read Dot's face the way some can read the weather . . . He was an Ordinary Seaman off a British Destroyer, who just happened to catch her at the right time. Or the wrong time, I should say, as it turned out. Though she didn't know that till two months later.

MARY:

Oh, God, Wiff, no . . .

WIFF:

She wasn't the first married woman it happened to during the War. Nor the first to seek out some quack. Dot said she could smell the liquor on him, and his hands shook. Those are facts, too.

MARY:

Stop it, Wiff. I don't want to hear any more . . .

WIFF:

No, but you're quick enough, Mary, to p'int the finger at me. Don't you t'ink I knows the guilt she feels for that one night in the boarding house? Or what she's suffered over the years for killing the child that was inside her? How bad will it get if she finds out that that's the reason she hasn't been able to conceive? That we might never have children now because of her mistake?

MARY: *beat*

I'm sorry, Wiff. Forgive me.

WIFF:

It's Dot I'm worried about, maid. It's a lot harder to forgive yourself.

> *NED enters briskly from the street and marches into the house, hanging up his windbreaker. He's wearing a black armband.*

NED: *entering the living room too self-absorbed and upset to notice the silence*

Well, I got to try out my new psychology, Jacob. I breezed into Arthur Murray's tonight, ready to ignore April for as long as it took. So guess what happened?

JACOB:

What?

NED:

She wasn't there, that's what happened. And you know who else wasn't there, Jacob?

JACOB:

Fred Noseworthy.

NED:

How'd you know that?

JACOB:

I'm smart.

155

MARY: *to NED, angrily*
Why are you wearing that black armband? We have
mourning enough in this house tonight! Take it off!

JACOB:
All right, don't jump on Ned. He's just trying to impress
April.   *To NED.*   If I was you, my son, I'd
get upstairs and finish that story I heard you scratching.

NED: *starts for the stairs*
I was just going to . . . Oh, and if April calls, tell her I'm
busy. On second thought, tell her I have a date.   *He
exits.*

> *JEROME and GRACE appear on the street and hurry up
> the steps. JEROME carries a bottle of Chivas Regal in a
> silver box. They enter the house and hang up their hats and
> coats.*

GRACE
Yahoo! We're here!

RACHEL: *returns from the kitchen*
We figured you'd forgotten all about us. What'd you do,
get lost?

JEROME: *enters the living room, followed by GRACE*
We're lucky to get here, Aunt Rachel. It was a madhouse
down around the Royal York.

GRACE:
Took forever to find a cab. When we did, the driver liked
to talk. And the more he talked the slower he drove.

JEROME:
His name was Horace Dockendorff. He even spelt it for
us.

GRACE:
Anyway, we're here. That's all that counts. The trouble
is, Mary, we can't stay for long. Just one quick drink.

MARY:
> Oh?

JACOB:
> One drink?

WIFF:
> What's the rush, Captain?

JEROME:
> I'm afraid duty calls, Sergeant. The paper just phoned;
> they want us to cover the banquet tonight at the Royal
> York.

GRACE:
> In fact, Horace is parked outside with his meter running,
> getting rich. He has strict orders to keep an eye on the
> time.   *Then.*   Where's Dot?

MARY:
> Dot's upstairs, Grace. She's not feeling well . . .

RACHEL:
> Jacob, where are your manners? Don't just stand there,
> get our guests a drink.

JACOB:
> What'll it be, folks? Scotch?

WIFF: *retrieves his glass*
> I'll do the honours, Jake. I could do with a shot myself
> right now.

JEROME: *hands WIFF the scotch*
> Open this, Sergeant. It's Chivas Regal.   *To*
> *JACOB.*   Compliments of the *Daily News*.

JACOB: *as WIFF goes to the sideboard*
> Chivas Regal, huh? In that case, sit down. Make
> yourselves at home.

RACHEL:

    Yes, tell us what you've been up to since we saw you last.
    Been keeping out of mischief?

JEROME:

    Well, I wrote the story yesterday, Aunt Rachel, and
    called it in. And Grace got the film off on the plane. The
    piece is called 'Elegy For A Nation.'

RACHEL:

    What's an elegy, my son?

JEROME:

    That's a mournful poem. A poem that laments the
    dead.   *MARY reacts.*   Like Thomas Gray's
    'Elegy Written in a Country Churchvard.'

    'Let not ambition mock their useful toil,
    Their homely joys, and destiny obscure;
    Nor grandeur hear with a disdainful smile
    The short and simple annals of the poor.'

        WIFF returns and hands GRACE and JEROME their
        drinks.

    'The boast of heraldry, the pomp of power,
    And all that beauty, all that wealth e'er gave
    Awaits alike the' inevitable hour:—
    The paths of glory lead but to the grave.'

MARY: *angrily*

    For God's sake, let's stop speaking of death, can't we?
    Some of us don't need to be reminded of that tonight! It's
    bad enough to look out the window and see that flag on
    the porch! It's bad enough the boarder comes home now
    with his mourning band! . . .

    An embarrassed silence.

JEROME:
>Look, Mary, I apologize if I've somehow upset you.
>Believe me, I hadn't the slightest intention . . .

JACOB:
>It's not you, Jerome. Mary's just not herself tonight.
>Isn't that so, Mary?

GRACE:
>I'm sorry to hear that.

RACHEL:
>I t'ink Jerome was only intending to explain, Mary,
>what . . .

MARY: *cutting in*
>I don't care, Aunt Rachel. This is not a house of
>mourning. This is not a wake. This is a simple house on a
>simple street, and death isn't welcome here. If there's any
>grieving to be done, let it be in the heart where it belongs.
>We don't need the trappings of grief for that.

JEROME:
>Some would disagree, Mary. There are black flags flying
>over Newfoundland this very minute. There are people
>right now sitting around their radios, knowing their lives
>are about to change. People who feel they had no real say
>in the matter. And yes, grief doesn't need to call attention
>to itself to be grief. And it doesn't need the trappings of
>grief to be real. But for those who can't speak, or won't,
>the sound of that flag in the wind may be all they need to
>say. And far more eloquent than words.

RACHEL:
>Amen.

JEROME:

I saw a man in Shearstown put his fist through a two-inch door the night of the referendum. You think our new Premier understands the sense of shame and betrayal that would make a man crush his hand to stop his heart from breaking?

GRACE:

That, Sergeant, is what English teachers call a rhetorical question.

JEROME:

Take Canada. How would the average Canadian feel if he climbed out of bed tomorrow and found he wasn't Canadian anymore? That Canada suddenly belonged to the United States? Christ, look what happened this morning, Grace. There's a prime example of what the future holds. You tell her.

GRACE:

Well, Mary, the Press was informed there'd be an official ceremony this morning on the steps of City Hall. They told us the Newfoundland flag would be lowered from the flagstaff, and the Canadian Ensign raised. All this to happen while the Mayor made his welcome speech to the new province.

JEROME:

They also informed us the 48th Highlanders Band would be there to play 'Ode to Newfoundland.' To cap it off, there'd be a fifteen-gun salute. Let's not forget that.

GRACE:

At 11:45 Mayor McCallum trots out to deliver his speech, all decked out in his Chain of Office and a big grin. Poor old Buck hardly had time to look solemn, did he, J.M.?

JEROME:
>No, because one minute later out troops George Weale, the city clerk, and informs one and all, including His Worship, that there's been a dreadful mistake, folks.

WIFF:
>A mistake?

JEROME:
>It turns out, Sergeant, that Buck has the wrong day. The ceremony's not till tomorrow morning, April the first.

RACHEL:
>His Worship couldn't wait, could he, to become the first April fool?

JEROME:
>You see, Mary, to the Mayor of Toronto the event was so trivial he couldn't bother to check his calendar. To that man in Shearstown it was a wound in the heart that might never heal. Speaking for myself, I knew we'd just had a glimpse of what it meant to be Canadian. Cheers.
>*He belts back his scotch.*

>>*BEN and BILLY come down the stairs, dressed once again as Goums, carrying their wooden rifles.*

BEN:
>Dad, it's ten past ten. Can we come down now? Can we, Mom?

GRACE:
>What are you two doing, sentry duty?

BILLY:
>We're Goums, Miss Wilcox.

JEROME:
>Remember what thieves those Goums were, Sergeant?

WIFF:

Yes, I took my boots off one night, and that's the last I saw of them. The CO told me they'd steal the hair off your head if they could.

RACHEL: *to herself*

I wouldn't pass comment on that, not if you paid me.

BEN:

Captain McKenzie, why is it you never wear your medals? Don't you want people to know how brave you are?

JACOB:

Good God, Ben, you don't ask questions like that of a man.

JEROME:

Medals don't mean much, Ben. A lot of brave men were never decorated. Like your Uncle Wiff there.

BILLY:

Like Dad, too?

BEN:

Dad wasn't brave, stupid. Didn't you hear what Granny said? He never even got overseas.

MARY:

And what does that make him in your eyes, Ben, less of a man that Captain McKenzie? Brave! Your father's as brave as any man in this room, and don't you forget it.

JACOB:

Don't be foolish, Mary. The only action I ever saw was that time we fired at a German sub off Bell Island. As it was, we missed.

MARY:
Is that how you judges courage, Jacob? By ribbons on a uniform? Is that what you wants your son to grow up believing? That that's how you measures a man's worth?

JACOB:
I didn't say that, did I?

MARY: *to BEN*
Why don't you ask your father what it's like to rise in the dark of winter and trudge off to work with his toolbox, to keep a roof over our heads and food on the table? Why don't you ask him how he feels if one of you gets a fever and he paces all night, pretending he's not tired? You t'ink for a minute he wouldn't give his life for either one of you?

BEN:
What are you getting mad at me for, Mom? I only meant . . .

MARY: *cutting in*
It's all right, my son. I'm not mad at you . . . I just wish you could've seen your father at Ned's age. He made all the young men back home pale by comparison. No offence, Jerome.

JEROME:
None taken, Mary . . .

MARY:
What do you suppose I saw in that man there, Ben? From the moment I decided to marry him I knowed there'd be no sable coats in my future. No expensive scotch whiskey in silver boxes. Those dreams belonged to another time . . . No, what I saw in your father from the first is what made him special. You see, I recognized that no odds what that man would always be there for me. Always be there for me and my kids. He'd sooner die first . . . *MARY is shaken by this admission.*

163

Slight Pause.

BILLY:
Dad, can I have a new bicycle?

MARY: *regaining her composure*
It takes courage to build a life, Ben. The courage to keep
on against all the odds. And in the long run it may be the
greatest courage of all . . . Now go on, take off that
fitout. You, too, Billy. There'll be no more Goums in this
house.

BILLY: *as he and BEN start for the stairs*
Dad, if I can't have a CCM bicycle, can I have a
catcher's mitt?

JACOB:
We'll see.

BILLY:
Oh, boy.

BEN: *to BILLY*
He's just saying that, dummy. Besides, you don't need a
new catcher's mitt.   *And they exit.*

Slight Pause.

MARY:
I suppose it's my turn now, Jerome, to apologize. As
Jacob said, I'm just not myself tonight . . .

GRACE:
Besides, you don't need to apologize, Mary.

JEROME:
No, I thought you were quite splendid just now. In fact,
very much yourself.

The taxi horn sounds.

GRACE:
> That'll be Horace, J.M. We'd better get a move on.

WIFF:
> Stay put, Captain, I'll get the coats.

MARY:
> Grace, I wish you didn't have to rush off like this. You scarcely had time to finish your drink.

GRACE:
> Perhaps another time Mary.

RACHEL:
> What'll you do tomorrow, maid? Fly home for the Big Event?

GRACE:
> No, we thought we'd take the train back. As it is, the plane won't arrive in time for the swearing-in ceremony.

JEROME:
> Not that we'll miss much. The Government wants to let the people get used to being Canadians. So most of the ceremonies won't be held till June. *WIFF returns with the coats. JACOB takes GRACE's coat and helps her on with it, while WIFF helps JEROME on with his.*
> Thanks, Sergeant.

RACHEL:
> Have a safe trip, you hear?

JEROME:
> Goodbye, Aunt Rachel. I'll send you the April 1st edition of the *Daily News*. You'll probably want it for a souvenir.

RACHEL:
> Souvenir, my foot. I'll frame it. I've never seen my name in print, let alone my picture.

JEROME: *shakes hands with JACOB*
Great to see you again, Jacob. Sorry we couldn't stay longer.

JACOB:
No odds. I'm glad you could make it, short as it was. It's meant a lot to us.

WIFF:
Dot'll be sorry she wasn't here, Captain. I'll give her your best.

JEROME:
Yes, do that . . . Well, goodbye, old friend.
Embraces him.   Good luck in the future.

WIFF:
T'anks, Captain. Same to you.

The taxi horn sounds again.

JEROME: *takes MARY's hand*
And last but not least . . . Goodbye, Mary Mercer. I want you to know I think your husband is a very lucky man.

RACHEL:
I'm sure my son would be the first to agree, wouldn't you, Jacob?

JACOB: *sheepishly*
I would, yes.

MARY:
You all heard that.

GRACE:
I think Mary's a lucky woman as well. I think you made that crystal clear tonight, Mary. Don't you agree J.M.?

166

JEROME: *to MARY*
I'm only sorry we don't see eye to eye on things political.
I don't suppose that's possible, is it?

MARY:
It's 1949, Jerome; the world is changing. How long could
an island go it alone? Sooner or later Newfoundland had
to be dragged into this day and age.

JEROME:
Maybe it did. But a country isn't just contained within its
borders, Mary. It's contained within its people. It's what
makes us special in our own eyes, and in the eyes of the
world. Losing that sense of who we are is a high price to
pay for comfort. Besides, who in Christ's name ever said
we had to have comfort above all else? *Who?* . . . Well,
goodbye, now. And God keep you all . . . Let's go,
Grace.

GRACE:
Goodbye! Goodbye, everyone!   *She and JEROME
disappear down the hall.*

JACOB:
There goes a good man, Wiff. I don't mind admitting
it . . .   *He crosses to the gramophone and begins to pick
through the records.*

JEROME and GRACE appear on the porch.

GRACE;
Don't you think a honeymoon on the train would be
romantic?

JEROME:
It takes three days to get married in this town.

GRACE;
Unless someone called your old friend, the Provincial
Secretary. He'd authorize the license in the morning.

JEROME:
You mean it, Grace?

GRACE: *starts to exit*
We could be married tomorrow morning at City Hall
before old Buck has a second stab at that speech of his.
DR. HUNTER starts down the stairs.

JEROME:
You realize, don't you, our anniversary would be April
the first?   *And he exits, following GRACE.*

WIFF:
How is she, Dan? Did you have a good heart to heart?

DR. HUNTER:
I mostly listened, Wiff. A doctor has to know when to do
that, too.

MARY:
Should I go up, Doctor?

DR. HUNTER:
No, she's pulling herself together. She'll be down . . .
     To WIFF.   In spite of all she's been through, I
still think your future may not be as bleak as you both
imagine. Why don't you and I discuss it while I break out
the champagne?   *He and WIFF start for the kitchen.*

RACHEL:
Don't be too long, Doctor. It's getting towards that
time . . .   *The doctor and WIFF exit. To MARY.*
     I suppose I'd better get down the good glasses.
*She crosses into the dining room where she takes the glasses from the
sideboard.*

     *JACOB puts a record on the gramophone, the kind you dance
     to, slowly.*

168

JACOB:
  The last time we danced under a full moon, Mary, was
  twenty-odd years ago. You ready for another twenty?

MARY:
  I'd sooner take it one day at a time, Jacob, like always.
  It's the only way to get there . . .   *She slips into his
  arms, and they dance, foreheads touching.*

          NED comes down the stairs, carrying a suitcase.

JACOB: *aware of NED, but still dancing*
  Where you off to, Ned? Trying to steal out without
  paying your rent?

NED:
  The suitcase belongs to Dot. She asked me to set it with
  the rest of her luggage.   *RACHEL sits in the alcove
  and listens in to the party line.*

MARY:
  Pay him no mind, Ned. Put it out on the porch.   *She
  grins at JACOB. NED exits onto the porch*   Did you see
  the look on his face?   *APRIL appears on the street.*

JACOB:
  I'll bet he t'inks he's the only one who ever danced this
  close.

          *NED appears on the porch, carrying the suitcase. When he
          sees APRIL, he slams the suitcase down beside the larger one.*

APRIL:
  What were you going to do, Ned, move out without
  telling me?

NED:
  Move out? The next move I make will be Debtor's
  Prison. Thanks to you I'm in hock for the rest of my life.
  And where the hell were you tonight?

APRIL:

None of your business.

NED:

Your mother told me you'd gone out to supper with
Tyrone Power's twin brother. What'd he do, look at
himself in your eyes all night?

APRIL:

Fred didn't take me; I took him. I saw no reason not to
invite him out, do you?

NED:

No, he's probably used to it. Oh, and in case you're
wondering, I haven't seen that woman since, and I don't
intend to. So goodnight.   *He starts for the front door.*

APRIL: *yells*

I hate you, Ned Spencer! I think I've always hated you!

NED: *whirls on her*

Well, I don't hate you! In fact, I love you! I've always
loved you! I think I loved you before I met you!

APRIL:

You did?

NED:

Not that it matters now. Goodnight.

APRIL:

Oh, but it does matter, Ned. I don't intend to go out with
anyone, either. I love your story, Ned. I think it's the
most beautiful story I've read in years.

NED:

You do?

APRIL:
> I read it in Lichee Gardens, waiting for Fred to show up.
> Then all through the meal I kept bursting into tears. Poor
> Fred. He kept telling me to stop it, everyone would think
> *he* had made me cry. Finally, I said, 'This isn't about *you*,
> Fred! Not everything is, you know!' And I threw my
> napkin in his face and ran out. Am I a terrible person,
> Ned? Am I?

NED:
> No, you're wonderful. You didn't pick up the check after
> all.

> *At that moment NORMAN hurries on from the street,*
> *followed by MISS DUNN who carries a tray of freshly*
> *baked scones. They hurry up the steps past the young lovers*
> *who barely acknowledge them.*

> *The gramophone record ends, and JACOB crosses to shut it*
> *off. NORMAN and MISS DUNN enter the house. NED*
> *and APRIL sit on the steps, heads together.*

MISS DUNN:
> We're back!

MARY:
> That didn't take long, Amelia.   *RACHEL hangs up*
> *the phone and crosses into the living room.*

MISS DUNN:
> Oh, Mr. Harris is an excellent chef, Mary. And a
> first-rate teacher. To be honest, Aunt Rachel, I had more
> trouble with his hands than I did with the scones.

RACHEL:
> I forgot to warn you. In any enclosed space never let him
> get behind you . . .   *MISS DUNN laughs and goes off*
> *to the kitchen. To NORMAN.*   I never should've
> introduced her to you. An old goat like you is no match
> for a lady like that.

NORMAN:

> Who said she's an old goat? She's a lovely warm woman, once you get to know her.

RACHEL:

> Norman, what did I ever to do deserve you? . . .

> > *NORMAN exits into the kitchen as DOT comes down the stairs, trailed by BEN and BILLY. She throws her coat over the banister.*

DOT:

> Stop picking on Norman, Aunt Rachel. After all, you pawned him off on Miss Dunn tonight . . . And don't everyone stare at me, I'm fine. Where's Wiff?

MARY:

> He's in the kitchen.   *The champagne cork explodes offstage.*

DOT:

> Wiff Roach, get your backside in here! Right now! *She crosses to the gramophone and winds it.*

> > *WIFF and DR. HUNTER enter from the kitchen, the doctor carrying the opened bottle of champagne. MISS DUNN trails behind, followed by NORMAN.*

WIFF:

> You wanted to see me, Dot?

DOT:

> Yes, I did, Wiff. I'm going to teach you the tango, my son. It's not a dance I can do alone. Or choose to. *She puts on the tango record.*

WIFF:

> I can't learn that, Dot.

DOT:

I'll teach you, if it kills me . . . *Takes his hand.*
Now to dance the tango, Wiff, you have to keep this
distance between us. See? . . . That means we don't ever
get any farther apart than this. Or any closer. You got
that?

WIFF:

So far, maid.

DOT:

The man always starts on his left foot forward. The
rhythm is slow-slow, quick-quick, slow. Let's see if you
can do that . . . *They do a few steps to make certain.*
Who said you couldn't learn? . . . All right, boy,
let's do it. Let's dance the tango, Wiff Roach. By the time
we finish we'll be Canadians.

RACHEL:

Then don't stop, maid! Keep right on dancing!

> *DOT and WIFF slip into the tango, hesitantly at first, then
> with a growing sense of confidence. DR. HUNTER
> watches a moment, then crosses to the dining room table and
> begins to pour the champagne. BEN and BILLY begin to
> clown, doing an imitation of their aunt and uncle.
> NORMAN and MISS DUNN also attempt the tango.
> JACOB, MARY, and RACHEL watch the dance with
> delight, while NED and APRIL, caught up in the music
> from inside the house, begin a more polished rendition on the
> street.*

> *The action freezes.*

ANNOUNCER:

'Ottawa, April the first. The King, in a message
conveyed to Viscount Alexander, today gave his blessing
to Confederation between Canada and Newfoundland.
His Majesty said, 'May the union that is now complete

173

continue, under God's guidance, to grow in strength, prosperity, and happiness, and may it bring new benefits to its people from sea to sea.'

The action unfreezes, and the dance goes on.

Curtain.